STUDIO FURNITURE

PALEY
1990

STUDIO FURNITURE

of the RENWICK GALLERY *Smithsonian American Art Museum*

Oscar P. Fitzgerald

Foreword by
Paul Greenhalgh

Smithsonian American Art Museum
Washington, D.C.

in association with Fox Chapel Publishing
East Petersburg, Pennsylvania

STUDIO FURNITURE
of the Renwick Gallery
Smithsonian American Art Museum

by Oscar P. Fitzgerald
Foreword by Paul Greenhalgh

Project Manager: Theresa Slowik
Editor: Tiffany D. Farrell
Designer: Karen Siatras
Researcher: Charlene Johnson
Proofreaders: M. Theresa Blackinton, Susan L. Efird

Cover: Michael Hurwitz, *Rocking Chaise*, 1989, Gift of Anne and Ronald Abramson, the James Renwick Alliance, and museum purchase made possible by the Smithsonian Institution Collections Acquisition Program (see pages 104–5)

Frontispiece: Albert Paley, *Lectern* (detail), 1990, Gift of Peter T. Joseph (see page 151)

Printed and bound in China

Library of Congress
Cataloging-in-Publication Data

Fitzgerald, Oscar P.
Studio Furniture of the Renwick Gallery, Smithsonian American Art Museum / Oscar P. Fitzgerald; foreword by Paul Greenhalgh.
p. cm.
Includes bibliographical references.

ISBN 978-1-56523-365-2 (hardcover)
ISBN 978-1-56523-367-6 (pbk.)

1. Studio furniture—United States—History—20th century—Catalogs.
2. Furniture—Washington (D.C.)—Catalogs.
3. Renwick Gallery—Catalogs. I. Smithsonian American Art Museum. II. Title.

NK2408.F62 2007
749.0973'074753—dc22

2007031007

1970 Broad Street
East Petersburg, PA 17520
www.FoxChapelPublishing.com

The Smithsonian American Art Museum is home to one of the largest collections of American art in the world. Its holdings—more than 41,000 works—tell the story of America through the visual arts and represent the most inclusive collection of American art in any museum today. It is the nation's first federal art collection, predating the 1846 founding of the Smithsonian Institution. The museum celebrates the exceptional creativity of the nation's artists whose insights into history, society, and the individual reveal the essence of the American experience.

The Renwick Gallery of the Smithsonian American Art Museum is dedicated to exhibiting American crafts and decorative arts from the nineteenth through the twenty-first centuries.

For more information or a catalogue of publications, write:

Office of Publications
Smithsonian American Art Museum
MRC 970, PO Box 37012
Washington, DC 20013-7012

Visit the museum's Web site at
AmericanArt.si.edu

Contents

7 Foreword
Paul Greenhalgh

10 Acknowledgments

13 Building the Collection

31 The Collection

205 A Statistical Snapshot of the Collection

217 Bibliography

Foreword

FURNITURE IS THE MOST OVERTLY FUNCTIONAL AND physical of all the arts. It keeps our bodies off the ground; it supports our repose; it provides our work surfaces; it stores and protects the stuff we eat and wear; and it protects and contains those precious things with which we choose to surround ourselves. It is core to our material existence.

But it is so much more. Furniture always has been a principal vehicle of human expression, from the earliest examples that have survived through the millennia up to the present. It has been a cultural signifier of prime importance, giving us indications as to the nature of the lives of those who made and used it. To look at ancient Egyptian or Chinese, eighteenth-century English, or nineteenth-century American Shaker furniture is to be presented with an essay on the social and spiritual mores of those peoples. It is an indicator of civilization.

Furniture is perhaps more allied to architecture than any of the other individual craft-based arts. It renders architecture useful in its normative functions, and it humanizes it. Some of the greatest furniture was designed by architects. Indeed, the reverse also is true. Robert Adam and Gerrit Rietveld, for example, provided the eighteenth and twentieth centuries respectively with seminal furnishings and buildings.

Apart from the heritage tying it to architecture, furniture has always been, and is, a freestanding art. And as such, it would in some senses be fair to say that as an art, it lost ground in the twentieth century. The loss was at least in part due to one of the most dominant philosophical positions on the production of modernist furniture, which insisted on focusing not on furniture as art, as a vehicle for individual and cultural expression, but on furniture as purely mechanical, as equipment for use in the domestic and work environments. Indeed, the whole world of ornamentation and decoration—as art—came under challenge in this period, and as such, furniture came under pressure to simplify its role in our culture.

It is in this regard that the role of the modern crafts has been vital. From the later nineteenth century, generation after generation of modern craftspeople struggled, against the functionalist trend, to maintain the possibility that furniture could be a medium for individual expression, as well as the conduit through which the history of furniture, and the people who created it, could be continually revisited. From the arts and crafts movement and the masters of art nouveau and the secession, through to the masters of the studio crafts movements of the later twentieth century, furniture has continued to serve as a medium for intellectual and emotional expression and as a vehicle for cultural memory.

I would say that after phenomenal development through the first half of the twentieth century, by 1970, America had become a dominant nation across much of craft practice. American ceramics and glass artists, for example, were absolutely core to the efflorescence of those practices

Stephen Courtney, *Secretarial Desk* (detail); see page 71.

into a sculptural, expressive, and dramatic new tradition. American jewelers took full part in the dramatic evolution that saw jewelry become a conceptually driven discourse. And fiber artists pushed textile art into wholly new realms.

The furniture world was, on the whole, less cohesive and dramatic than these other genres and unfolded in a more subtle and complex way. It never had a movement. There is no one cohesive school or intellectual thrust in American furniture making, but rather, a number of seams of activity. Some makers remained broadly loyal to what might be termed the arts-and-crafts tradition, at its most powerful in the later nineteenth and early twentieth century; others effectively combined wood carving with furniture to forge a more sculptural practice; some used popular and folk imagery to make witty and cryptic comments on life; some blended in with mainstream design; and yet others developed conceptual approaches that questioned the very nature of furniture itself. It has been a rich diversity, and one that can be collectively assessed only with rigorous and patient scholarship. That is where this book comes in.

The Renwick Gallery's studio furniture collection is a vital resource for the study and appreciation of American furniture. The eighty-four examples catalogued here constitute one of the most important American collections. Like all museum collections, and of course museums themselves, there is often little in the way of logic in the initial founding impetus. Vacated by the U.S. Court of Claims, the historic building that is now the Renwick Gallery lay vacant until First Lady Jacqueline Kennedy advocated a viable program and purpose for it. The government then transferred the building to the Smithsonian Institution.

When the Renwick Gallery was formed in 1972, it had no mandate to build a collection. Beginning in the mid-1980s, under the leadership of National Museum of American Art Director Charles Eldredge, the Renwick formed a policy to collect. From then on, it did so with intelligence and gusto.

Studio Furniture is a seminal contribution to furniture literature. It seems to me that above all else it does three things. First, it is an absolutely vital resource for the history of modern American furniture makers. The biographies and bibliographies of these central makers provide the student, collector, and educated layperson with the foundation for study. Second, taken as a whole, the volume is a concise history of modern American furniture practice. Third, the catalogue is a brilliant institutional history of American craft.

Modern American furniture makers have been open and experimental with regard to diverse materials. Many practice with metal, fiber, plastic, and found materials. Nevertheless, at the core of the furniture genre is wood. And in the twentieth century, that has been the single greatest contribution of the American masters. In a nation blessed with extraordinary supplies of the raw material and émigrés from rich furniture-making countries, the environment for a continuing tradition of expressive wooden furniture was always here. Accordingly, as these pages reveal, the tradition of wooden furniture has been maintained and pushed into wholly new terrain. The range is remarkable—from the raw expressiveness of Garry Knox Bennett to the breathtaking exactitude of Wendell Castle; from the virtuosity of John Cederquist to the eclectic, adjusted traditionalism of Daniel Mack; from the classic seriousness of Wharton Esherick to the subversiveness of Jacob Cress.

Perhaps this returns me to my earlier point. Furniture is simultaneously the most functional and physical of craft media, but it is also redolent with conceptual, historiographic, and individual narrative. Perhaps more than any other group internationally during the last fifty years, the American artists chronicled in *Studio Furniture* have reminded us such narratives always have been part of the furniture universe. We owe them much.

Paul Greenhalgh
Director, The Corcoran Gallery of Art
Washington, D.C.

Acknowledgments

THE AUTHOR'S NAME APPEARS ON THE TITLE PAGE, but no book is possible without the help of countless friends and colleagues who contribute in both small and large ways to make it a reality. First and foremost is Charlene Johnson, who completed the daunting task of compiling the bibliography and biographical sketches that bring to life each of the artists represented in the Renwick collection. As a student, collector, scholar, and studio artist in her own right, Johnson has been a constant advisor, reader, and friend without whom this project might never have been completed.

The research really began with my spring 2003 Studio Furniture class at the Smithsonian Institution/Parsons School of Design masters program in the decorative arts. Several of my students that semester interviewed artists in the Renwick collection about their work. The students included Christian Chute, Marcee Craighill, Samira Farmer, Kate Hughes, Pam Lict, Kate Livie, April Pride, Virginia Waring, and Betsy Davison. Davison and Allison Byrd completed similar assignments in subsequent classes. As part of an independent study project, Kyra Swanson identified all of the furniture makers who received National Endowment for the Humanities awards.

I am grateful to the James Renwick Alliance for awarding me a research fellowship in 2004 that allowed me to begin my study of the collection and for encouraging my work ever since. I am particularly grateful to past presidents John Kotely and Diane Grainer, and to former vice president Marc Grainer, for their unstinting support and advice. The fellowship allowed me to conduct telephone interviews with the artists, and that information forms the basis for the catalogue entries. Each artist generously reviewed my draft for accuracy.

I am particularly indebted to the staff of the Renwick Gallery and the Smithsonian American Art Museum (SAAM) for the countless hours they have lavished on this project. Without the Renwick artist files, it would have been difficult to complete this book. The custodian of the invaluable records is Marguerite Hergesheimer, who tolerated repeated interruptions to provide details whenever I asked. Robyn Kennedy, the administrator of the Renwick, and her assistant, Rebecca Robinson, always were there to offer ongoing support and encouragement.

The manuscript benefited immeasurably from the diligent and careful editing by Tiffany Farrell, the finest editor with whom I have had the pleasure of working. The book is far better as a result of her hard work. Words are important, but the layout and design by Karen Siatras also is critical for understanding and appreciating the work. Richard Sorensen, the keeper of the images, also was indispensable in locating photography of the furniture. Much of the collection was expertly photographed by Bruce Miller, a project supported by a grant from the James Renwick Alliance. SAAM staff photographers Gene Young and Mildred Baldwin also provided stunning shots.

To Betsy Broun and Rachel Allen, the director and deputy director of SAAM, I extend special thanks for supporting this catalogue from the very beginning and making it happen. Having been personally involved with the Renwick from its early years, Broun offered many invaluable insights only first-hand experience could provide.

I want to especially thank the former curators-in-charge of the Renwick—Lloyd Herman, Michael Monroe, and Kenneth Trapp—and former curator Jeremy Adamson, for reading my manuscript and offering many helpful comments and suggestions that have enabled me to write an accurate and clear history of the collection.

Colleagues at other institutions graciously provided lists of studio furniture in their charge as a comparison to the Renwick collection. The colleagues included Pat Warner at the Museum of Fine Arts, Boston; Kristin Watts at the Mint Museum in Charlotte, North Carolina; and Thomas Michie at the Rhode Island School of Design.

Several gallery owners have provided much appreciated advice, including Louis Wexler of Wexler Gallery, Rick Snyderman of Snyderman Gallery in Philadelphia, and Vena Sengh at Sansar Gallery in Bethesda, Maryland. These longtime stalwarts in the field provided invaluable perspectives. Andrew Glasgow, the executive director of the Furniture Society, also offered continuing encouragement and support.

Finally, I am indebted to John Kelsey for introducing me to Fox Chapel Publishing and to Alan Giagnocavo, the president, both of whom have been enthusiastic about *Studio Furniture* from the beginning.

Throughout it all, my wife, Toby, showed remarkable forbearance as I struggled with the manuscript and the publication process. She was even persuaded to read a few drafts and offered many helpful suggestions.

I am encouraged that a new generation of collectors has begun to discover the work of studio furniture makers. Although my daughter, Molly, leads a peripatetic life in the field of international public health, she appreciates fine craftsmanship and design. My son, Michael, a university chemistry professor, has begun to furnish his home with studio furniture. Even my granddaughters, Madeline and Emily, seem to delight in our fledgling studio furniture collection. It is to my family and the new generation of studio furniture enthusiasts that this book is dedicated.

BUILDING THE COLLECTION

THE EIGHTY-FOUR PIECES OF STUDIO FURNITURE OWNED BY THE RENWICK GALLERY OF THE Smithsonian American Art Museum constitute one of the largest assemblages of American studio furniture in the nation. Three former administrators—Lloyd Herman, Michael Monroe, and Kenneth Trapp—amassed a seminal collection that samples studio furniture's great diversity. From the carefully crafted stools of Tage Frid to the art deco chest painted by Rob Womack, from the one-of-a-kind *Ghost Clock* sculpture by Wendell Castle, to the limited production stool by David Ebner, the collection documents the astonishing variety of the American studio furniture movement. From first-generation makers such as Wharton Esherick and Sam Maloof, who emphasized technique and the beauty of wood, to second-generation artists like John Cederquist and Alphonse Mattia, who transformed their furniture into narrative and sculpture, the field is well covered.

Lloyd Herman and the Nascent Studio Furniture Collection

LIKE THE MODERN CRAFT MOVEMENT ITSELF, THE RENWICK GALLERY IS RELATIVELY YOUNG. It traces its formation to the 1960s, when the U.S. Court of Claims had vacated the historic building, named for its nineteenth-century architect James Renwick. Proposals to demolish the building followed. However, First Lady Jacqueline Kennedy, dedicated to the restoration of Lafayette Park and its surrounding buildings, advocated for its preservation. Ultimately, the architectural gem was transferred to the Smithsonian Institution in 1965 and became part of the National Collection of Fine Arts (NCFA).

Lloyd E. Herman, the director of the Office of Exposition Hall Programs, the short-lived name given to the changing exhibition program in the Smithsonian's Arts and Industries Building in the late 1960s, had written a memo recommending that the newly acquired Renwick be turned into "The Renwick Design Center."[1] Taking up Herman's idea, Dillon Ripley, then secretary of the Smithsonian Institution, persuaded President Lyndon Johnson that the Renwick be used "as a gallery of arts, crafts, and design."[2] In 1971, Herman was appointed the Renwick's first director. Although he had no formal training in craft or design, few other museum professionals had a craft background at that time because of the paucity of academic programs in the field.

After a renovation designed by renowned architect Hugh Jacobsen, the Renwick Gallery opened to the public in January 1972 with eight inaugural exhibitions.

John Eric Byers, *Hat Box Chest* (detail); see page 45.

Herman himself curated the primary show, *Woodenworks: Furniture Objects by Five Contemporary Craftsmen,* which featured Arthur Espenet Carpenter, Wendell Castle, Wharton Esherick, Sam Maloof, and George Nakashima. *Woodenworks* showcased fifty pieces by leaders of the first generation of studio furniture makers. All of the artists would subsequently figure prominently in the gallery's permanent collection.[3] Before he retired in 1986, Herman mounted more than one hundred exhibitions, almost one-third featuring individual craft artists both American and foreign. At the outset, however, forming a permanent collection was not part of the plan.[4]

Unaware the Renwick Gallery was created as a venue for temporary exhibits, private donors occasionally offered the museum craft objects. Herman dutifully referred donors to the Smithsonian's Cooper-Hewitt National Design Museum in New York City or to the Ceramics and Glass Department of the National Museum of American History, neither of which was prepared to accept such pieces. Herman and Joshua C. Taylor, the director of the National Collection of Fine Arts, finally decided the objects were too important to pass up, so Herman began accepting a few. The NCFA, of which the Renwick was a part, had already acquired several craft objects even before the Renwick opened, most from the touring exhibition *Objects: USA,* a show sponsored by the S. C. Johnson & Son Company that premiered at NCFA in 1968. When the exhibition ended after an international tour, the company distributed the objects to various museums including NCFA. Starting with a small core, Herman added to the craft collection on a limited basis into the 1980s.

An important early exhibition that contained studio furniture was *Craft Multiples,* mounted in 1975 following a national competition. Herman's idea was to feature alternatives to unique sculptural objects. He chose works created in editions of at least ten that also appealed to the spirit and enriched daily life. Shinichi Miyazaki, who submitted a chair for the show, summed up the ideals of many craftsmen when he said, "When skills are applied to the proper materials, the result is unique and artistic to a degree impossible to obtain by mass production. And when we use such furniture, the craftsman's joy in creation is somehow communicated to us and we partake of it."[5] In the end, a three-person jury selected 133 objects from about five thousand applicants. *Craft Multiples* traveled around the country for three years after closing at the Renwick. A $40,000 grant from Susan and Timothy Mellon enabled

Herman to purchase about half of the objects from this exhibition. Of the sixty-three objects acquired, nine furniture pieces formed the basis of a fledgling studio furniture collection.

Several of the inaugural pieces were submitted by craftsmen who would later become leaders in the field. Objects included a music stand by Wendell Castle, a wall unit by John Cederquist, and a stool by David Ebner. Castle's music stand represents the early work of a craftsman who went on to reinvent himself numerous times over his career. Without the provenance, it would be impossible to know simply by looking that the wall unit was created by John Cederquist. Soon after making the cabinet, Cederquist moved from art-deco-inspired casework to his familiar trompe l'oeil creations. Ebner's stool was the prototype for what soon emerged as his signature piece, one he produces in bronze as well as wood.

After the *Craft Multiples* acquisitions, Herman added only three more pieces of studio furniture during his directorship. The 1950 desk by Wharton Esherick was perhaps the most significant, even though in the 1970s, Esherick's importance in the field was not widely appreciated. Herman actually used it as his desk. Now, however, Esherick is acknowledged as the patriarch of the studio furniture movement. The second piece, a chair—really a fiber sculpture—donated by the artist Norma Minkowitz, represented an important precursor to trends in the studio furniture field in the 1980s and 1990s, when many makers began to produce pieces that were more artistic than functional. Just before his retirement, Herman acquired the signature *Throne Chair* by Robert Whitley, whose Windsor chair had already been acquired from the *Craft Multiples* show.

After he left, Herman donated two notable pieces to the museum. When *Woodenworks* closed, Herman attempted to buy George Nakashima's *Conoid Chair* for his personal collection, but the artist insisted on giving it to him instead. Soon after Nakashima died in 1990, Herman presented *Conoid Chair* to the museum. Herman also had bought a prototype, production model of the *Molded Plywood Chair* by Washington, D.C.-area artist and industrial designer Peter Danko. In 1995, after Danko had achieved national prominence, Herman donated that piece to the museum as well. The gift honored Michael Monroe, Herman's former curator and his successor as chief, upon Monroe's retirement.

The Renwick Gallery Becomes the Nation's Craft Museum

BY THE MID-1980S, IT BECAME CLEAR THAT COLLECTING CRAFT OBJECTS WOULD FORM an integral part of the museum's mission. At that time, several events resulted in the Renwick's focusing its mission on collecting and promoting craft. When the National Collection of Fine Arts was renamed the National Museum of American Art (NMAA) by an Act of Congress in 1980, its focus became solely American art. Even though the Renwick's early exhibitions were international in scope, its nascent collection had already been limited to American craft. Charles Eldredge, who became director of the NMAA in 1982 after the unexpected death of Taylor a year earlier, codified the emphasis on American art in the NMAA and on American craft at the Renwick. Eldredge also decided the Renwick Gallery should include all of the same programs as other curatorial departments, including exhibitions, research and publications, public programs, and collections. The last element marked a dramatic policy shift, one that charged the Renwick's curators with acquiring the very best examples of American craft for the permanent collection.

In the late 1980s, as the new acquisition policy got underway, a support group helped fund purchases. The James Renwick Collectors Alliance (renamed the James Renwick Alliance in 1987) had been created in 1982. Moved by Lloyd Herman's comment that he was having trouble finding funds for public programs, Charles Gailis—then a trustee of the Haystack Mountain School of Crafts in Deer Isle, Maine—facilitated the establishment of an ad hoc committee of local collectors and others interested in craft to investigate establishing a support group. The by-laws charged the new organization to support programs at the Renwick Gallery and also "to establish permanent collections of American crafts of artistic significance and superior workmanship."[6] At first, the group wanted to support American crafts on a national basis, but eventually it became committed to supporting the Renwick exclusively. Beginning in 1985, the Renwick Alliance focused on raising money for acquisitions. In 1987, members were granted the right to vote on new acquisitions.

However, by the late 1980s, the Renwick faced an uncertain future. When Herman retired in 1986, the position of director was abolished because it was determined there should not be two directors within the same organization. About the same time, Robert McCormick Adams, secretary of the Smithsonian Institution, mused in public that every aspect of the Smithsonian, including the purpose and use of the Renwick, should be open to question. The statement unleashed a flurry of suggestions. Some in the Smithsonian's National Museum of American History wanted to take over the Renwick as a concert hall and gallery for the historical musical instrument collection. Because of its proximity to the White House, others proposed an exhibition space for objects relating to the First Ladies. Still others wanted to commandeer the museum to serve as a showcase for the Smithsonian Institution Traveling Exhibition Service. Many advocates within the NMAA and the Renwick Gallery, including Elizabeth Broun, who had been NMAA's assistant director and chief curator since 1983, lobbied tenaciously to protect and promote the fledgling craft museum. In addition, the Renwick Alliance mobilized support. As a result, Secretary Adams authorized a Visiting Craft Committee to make recommendations on the future of the Renwick.

The committee not only advised that the Renwick should continue to exhibit American craft, but also that it should build a nationally recognized craft collection representing the best works and makers in the nation. It also recommended the curator-in-charge, the new name for the administrator, should report to the director of NMAA rather than to the NMAA's chief curator, as had been the case previously. The committee went as far as suggesting the Renwick be established as a separate museum, but recognized budgetary and political considerations made that impractical at the time.

Acquisition of Studio Furniture Icons

THE MOST NOTICEABLE CHANGE AS A RESULT OF THE VISITING CRAFT COMMITTEE'S recommendations was Michael W. Monroe, who became the new curator-in-charge in 1986, began to develop a systematic collecting policy. A graduate of the Cranbrook Academy of Art in Bloomfield Hills, Michigan, Monroe had served as curator of the Renwick under Herman for twelve years and previously as a director of a university art gallery. Monroe began to identify important objects for the collection and cultivated the support of the Renwick Alliance.

Meanwhile, Charles Eldredge at the NMAA arranged, against all odds, to include the Renwick in the Smithsonian-wide Collections Acquisition Program. Consequently, in 1988, the gallery received a quarter of a million dollars for acquisitions, provided that half of the funds were matched by outside benefactors. Eldredge's initiative

Lloyd E. Herman (left) directed the Renwick Gallery from 1971 until 1986. He was succeeded by curator-in-charge Michael W. Monroe (right).

provided a tremendous windfall, as excellent craft objects could be acquired for reasonable prices. When Elizabeth Broun became NMAA's director in 1989, she continued to support the Renwick with acquisition funds. The Renwick Alliance enthusiastically answered appeals to match the challenge grant. Benefiting from the efforts, Monroe was able to add twenty-two objects to the studio furniture collection. Five of these were purchased jointly by the Smithsonian and the Renwick Alliance.

After succeeding Herman, Monroe did not initially focus on studio furniture. However, early in his tenure at the museum he witnessed a confluence of maturing young talent and extraordinary ideas—a contagious energy. He then felt a sense of urgency to capture that energy. Monroe recognized that following the 1972 *Woodenworks* show and the establishment of the Program in Artisanry at Boston University in 1975, interest in studio furniture had blossomed. He wanted to capture the possibilities inherent in the moment, while it was still possible to acquire significant pieces by emerging artists. Having seen in other craft fields the increasing inaccessibility of works by leading artists as their reputations soared, Monroe was determined to collect such pieces of studio furniture before they became unattainable.

Knowing storage space was at a premium, he sought to acquire few but choice pieces. With a list of important makers in his pocket, he assiduously perused craft literature and frequented galleries in search of the most representative examples. Also in the back of Monroe's mind was the quest for diversity in both artists and forms. If all the collection were to be displayed, he wanted to see more than just chairs, for example. Moreover, he did not feel comfortable commissioning work because the result might not truly reflect the artist's full potential.

In 1989, Monroe added the most impressive object to the collection, Wendell Castle's *Ghost Clock*, one of the few works that has been continuously displayed in the permanent gallery. Created by arguably the foremost craftsman in the field, the sculpture represented a turning point in Castle's career. The piece, *Ghost Clock*, had initially starred in the *Masterpieces of Time* exhibition, which debuted at the Taft Museum in Cincinnati in the fall of 1985. Alexander F. Milliken, who promoted Wendell Castle's work during the 1980s, had suggested the project to Castle several years earlier. *Masterpieces of Time*, featuring thirteen clocks, then traveled to the

Kenneth Trapp followed Michael Monroe as the Renwick Gallery's curator-in-charge beginning in 1995.

Alexander F. Milliken Gallery in New York before opening at the Renwick in December 1985 for a four-month run.[7]

The exhibition was Castle's first body of work that represented a more conceptual and sculptural approach. For Monroe, the clocks epitomized the blurring of the traditional distinction between craft and sculpture, a trend that swept the studio furniture field in the 1980s and 1990s. Although Monroe coveted the clock from the moment he saw it, it took four years of torturous negotiations before the deal was concluded. In the end, Monroe felt it was one of his most rewarding acquisitions. Along with Albert Paley's *Portal Gates*, *Ghost Clock* has become an icon in the gallery and a favorite among visitors.

Despite the work Monroe lavished on that acquisition, he did not neglect other second-generation furniture craftsmen. He had an opportunity to evaluate over an extended period the work of many of these artists when the landmark *New American Furniture* exhibition—which was organized by the Museum of Fine Arts, Boston in 1989—traveled to the Renwick Gallery.[8] Monroe was able to acquire three pieces from the show—Jere Osgood's *Cylinder-Front Desk*, Garry Knox Bennett's *Boston Kneehole*, and Michael Hurwitz's *Rocking Chaise*. Additionally, he went on to collect furniture by seven other makers represented in the exhibition. One piece from the show by Rick Wrigley got away, but the Renwick Alliance would commission and fund an almost identical one twelve years later (*The Rick Wrigley Renwick Cabinet*). Remarkably, the Renwick Gallery would eventually acquire works by fourteen of the twenty-five makers represented in this seminal exhibition.

One reason the exhibition had such an impact was the excellent catalogue and essay by the curator Edward S. Cooke Jr. The catalogue represented the first scholarly appraisal of the field and showcased some of the best young talent. In his essay, Cooke explored the shift in the field from the first to the second generation. About half of the makers featured in the catalogue—such as John Dunnigan, Timothy Philbrick, Jere Osgood, and Rick Wrigley—represented young makers who followed closely in the footsteps of the first generation; the other half represented the new wave, or the second generation. Rosanne Somerson, Tommy Simpson, Alphonse Mattia, and others believed in fine craftsmanship but were not as enamored with the beauty of the unadorned wood. They saw their furniture as canvases to be painted and invested with meaning, as in the fine art realm.

Nevertheless, about half of the twenty-two pieces of furniture Monroe collected were made by craftsmen from the first generation. *Conoid Chair* and *Conoid Bench* by George Nakashima, *Double Rocking Chair* and *Pedestal Table* by Sam Maloof, and Tage Frid's signature *Three Three-Legged Stools* represent work by three of the most important and influential members of a group that placed the highest value upon technique and wood. In addition to the first generation of makers, Monroe collected a desk by Jere Osgood, who signaled a transition between the first generation's emphasis on fine craftsmanship and beautiful wood and the second generation, who emphasized design.

Daniel Jackson, a colleague of Osgood's at Boston University's Program in Artisanry, also served as a bridge between the two generations. The purchase of Jackson's *Four Step Library Ladder* illustrated Monroe's sophisticated knowledge of the field. Although Jackson had a relatively short career, he made a lasting impact. Teaching first at the Philadelphia College of Art and then at the newly established Program in Artisanry, Jackson influenced some of the most acclaimed makers of the second generation. He urged his students, including Alphonse Mattia, to see furniture as more than a craft challenge and helped free them to make some of the most creative furniture of the era. Consequently, when a dealer offered Jackson's ladder to the Renwick Gallery, Monroe immediately accepted it. Guided by his knowledge of the field and his aesthetic sensibility, Monroe systematically implemented the Renwick's mission to collect the very best of American craft. His choices clearly set the Renwick on a solid path to becoming the nation's showcase for American studio furniture.

Support from Galleries, Corporations, and the James Renwick Alliance

PETER JOSEPH, A COLLECTOR AND WEALTHY FINANCIER, WAS DEEPLY IMPRESSED BY THE *New American Furniture* show—so much that in 1991, he established the Peter Joseph Gallery in New York City to showcase the best work in the studio furniture field. During its short life, the gallery propelled studio furniture into high art. Joseph represented many of the artists from the *New American Furniture* show, a factor that contributed to their notoriety—and the increasing value of their work. Joseph understood the importance of national recognition for his stable of artists. To help garner that attention, he, along with the Pritam and Eames Gallery in East Hampton, Long Island, donated Thomas Hucker's signature *Low Table* to the Renwick Gallery in 1991, the year Joseph's showroom opened.

After leaving the Renwick in 1995, Monroe went to work for Peter Joseph. When Joseph's health declined and he had to close the gallery in 1996, Monroe suggested that rather than selling the collection, Joseph should distribute important pieces to appropriate museums to serve as a legacy for his support of the craft movement. Joseph's widow carried through on this suggestion, and as a result, the Renwick acquired a lectern by Albert Paley, *Points of Reference* by Alphonse Mattia, and *Desk with Clock 2* by Wendell Castle. Since Joseph's death in 1996, few galleries have been able to sustain the high level of interest in studio furniture that Joseph's business generated.

In 1997, two other galleries that specialized in studio furniture made substantial donations to the museum. Leo Kaplan Modern in New York, which represented Richard Ford, donated *Uncle Rick's Wonderland.* Franklin Parrasch, who opened Mogul Gallery in Washington, D.C., in 1986 and three years later moved to New York, wanted to showcase studio furniture in a fine arts context. His gallery, along with a private donor, presented Bob Trotman's *Louise* to the Renwick. Parrasch and the anonymous benefactor had intended to donate a different artwork called *Sybil,* but when it arrived damaged, Parrasch arranged with local collectors Diane and Marc Grainer to swap *Sybil* for *Louise.* But for these circumstances, one of the most evocative pieces would not have come into the collection.

In the early 1990s, the Renwick received support from an unlikely source. At that time, MCI Communications approached the museum about forming a craft collection, and agreed to give the NMAA the right of first refusal to acquire any gifts from the collection. MCI's world headquarters was just around the corner from the Renwick, and Michael Monroe and Kenneth R. Trapp, who would follow Monroe as curator-in-charge, worked closely with the corporation to implement the project. Having introduced several important artists to MCI, including Peter Pierobon, John Cederquist, and Stephen Perrin, Monroe was pleased to hear in 2001 that three of their pieces came to the museum shortly before the company (which had merged with WorldCom in 1998) went bankrupt. These included Pierobon's *Time Totem,* Cederquist's *Kimono to Go,* and Perrin's *Folding Wall Chairs.*

Notwithstanding the support from galleries and private donors, some of the most noteworthy furniture in the collection was acquired with the help of funds from the Renwick Alliance. Between its founding in 1982 and 1997, the Alliance voted to support the acquisition of 102 objects, of which twelve were furniture. One highlight proposed by Monroe was John Cederquist's *Ghost Boy* cabinet (similar to the piece Cederquist made for the *New American Furniture* exhibition). Longtime Alliance members Anne and Ronald Abramson matched money from the acquisition fund to secure its purchase. On at least four other occasions during this period, the Smithsonian-wide Collections Acquisition Fund augmented money from the Renwick Alliance to permit adding important furniture to the collection.

In 1992, Monroe hired Jeremy Adamson as curator. Having a doctorate in art history from the University of Michigan, Adamson was the first full-time staff member to produce major scholarly catalogues for the Renwick Gallery. Adamson immediately organized an exhibition on American wicker in 1993 and published a catalogue to go with it.[9] Although no wicker furniture was acquired for the museum as a result of the exhibition, the book set a high standard for future scholarly publications initiated by the Renwick.

The Kenneth Trapp Era

IN OCTOBER 1995, KENNETH TRAPP, FORMER CURATOR OF DECORATIVE ARTS AT THE Oakland Museum of California, became the Renwick's second curator-in-charge. Two years later, he celebrated the twenty-fifth anniversary of the Renwick with *Renwick at 25*, an exhibition of 101 objects from the collections representing all media. A catalogue titled *Skilled Work* was published to coincide with the show. It highlighted treasures from the collection, including furniture such as Judy Kensley McKie's *Monkey Settee*, Wendell Castle's *Ghost Clock*, John Cederquist's *Ghost Boy*, Tom Loeser's *Four by Four*, Alphonse Mattia's *Points of Reference*, John Dunnigan's *Slipper Chairs*, Michael Hurwitz's *Rocking Chaise*, Sam Maloof's *Low-Back Side Chair*, Garry Knox Bennett's *Boston Kneehole*, and Jere Osgood's *Cylinder-Front Desk*.

Unlike many curators of major museums who focus solely on collecting works by established icons, Trapp made a conscious effort to acquire promising, midcareer work by emerging makers, with notable success. One way to define the category is to assume the average career lasts about thirty years; the midpoint is then fifteen years.[10] Six artists Trapp added to the collection—David Chapman, Rainer Facklam, Douglas Finkel, Jenna Goldberg, David Merrifield, and Stephen Perrin—were in the midcareer category.[11]

If the definition is broadened to include a ten-year career midpoint, the list of artists expands to a total of fifteen, including Jim Rose, Stephen Courtney, Richard Ford, Paul Freundt, Joanne Shima, Charles Radtke, Robert Bliss, John Eric Byers, and Peter Pierobon—all of whom started working professionally in 1985 or later. Trapp added work by all these makers to the collection.[12]

When considering the execution date, the furniture of forty makers was finished less than fifteen years into their professional careers.[13] Excluding the three pieces obtained from MCI and nine iconic pieces acquired with the help of the Renwick Alliance, two-thirds of the work Trapp added to the collection represented midcareer or earlier examples. In contrast, only about one-third of the furniture Monroe collected could be defined by the same term. Overall, mature and midcareer work is about evenly balanced in the collection, with midcareer slightly favored at 52 versus 48 percent.[14] Thus, Trapp's philosophy remains highly visible in the collection today.

Trapp made a conscious effort to avoid the "one-of-each" and the "copycat" approaches—an all-too-common institutional obsession with collecting one representative example of only the currently fashionable makers. Heading a federal institution, he wanted to seek out not just established artists, but a more diverse group of young makers who demonstrated potential. Like virtually all museum directors, he was limited by available funds as well as suitable objects. For example, he would like to have acquired a more representative willow piece from David Chapman, but one was not available. While Trapp believed it would have been ideal to evaluate an artist's complete oeuvre after his or her death, that approach was rarely possible.

Although Trapp sought out artists with good design sense first and foremost, he was particularly drawn to artists working in nontraditional materials. As an example of Trapp's preference for strong design, he acquired Charles Radtke's *Sarcophagus Cabinet # 1*, which has a decidedly arts-and-crafts feel in its form and proportions. The combination of steel and wood was probably what attracted Trapp to David Merrifield's *Tea Cabinet*, which he saw while jurying the 2002 *Washington Craft Show*. After it won best in show, Trapp persuaded the Smithsonian Women's Committee, the Renwick Alliance, and several other donors to purchase it for the museum. In acquiring works by Jim Rose and Paul Freundt, Trapp liked the idea that they eschewed wood altogether and executed furniture all in steel.

Trapp is justifiably proud of his legacy of studio furniture in the Renwick's collection. He helped acquire fifty-five pieces, just over two-thirds of the total number of objects. He is particularly pleased with Timothy Philbrick's *Curly Cherry Cellaret.* Trapp did not hesitate to act when Kim Schmahmann's *Bureau of Bureaucracy* also suddenly became available after Jonathan Fairbanks, curator at the Museum of Fine Arts, Boston, recommended the Renwick as the most suitable repository for the monumental piece. When leading tours, Trapp relished the pleasure of showing off the intricacies of this extraordinarily complex cabinet.

Not all of Trapp's acquisitions were ideal. He admits the dysfunctional pull on the Stephen Courtney *Secretarial Desk* always bothered him, but he was willing to overlook that small flaw because of the creative design, which combined traditional maple with copper leaf, copper-plated cast bronze, glass, leather, and golf tees. Trapp also believed the overlarge proportions of the Renwick's example of Robert Erickson's *Floating Back Rocker* were quirky, but when it became available, he seized the opportunity to add work by the up-and-coming craftsman to the collection.[15]

Sculpture and Jewelry by Furniture Makers

TRAPP ALSO REPRESENTED SOME FURNITURE ARTISTS NOT BY THEIR FURNITURE BUT BY their sculpture or jewelry. Although such pieces are not included in this catalogue, their presence enriches the collection and merits mention. For example, Jon Brooks trained at the Rochester Institute of Technology under Wendell Castle and started fashioning furniture from large blocks of wood in the manner of Howard Werner and J. B. Blunk. During a one-year residency at the University of Tasmania, Brooks was exposed to aboriginal art. As a result, Brooks started fashioning found wood into ladders, ladder-back chairs, and stick figures. The Renwick's *Pathless Resistance* sculpture explores the ladder theme that pervades much of his furniture.

Mark Sfirri of Philadelphia is best known for his eccentric turnings, which he demonstrates in his furniture and other pieces. The Renwick's collection includes his well-known wall sculpture *Rejects from the Bat Factory.* Frank E. Cummings III of Los Angeles, California, is recognized for his turnings, as well as jewelry and handmade clocks. The Renwick owns one of Cummings's turned vessels. In addition to Peter Pierobon's *Time Totem* clock, the museum also has a turned mahogany, wall-hung disk by him called *A Long Life May Not Be Good Enough, But a Good Life Is Long Enough.*

Albert Paley, *Pendant*, 1973. Gift of the James Renwick Alliance and museum purchase through the Smithsonian Institution Collections Acquisition Program, 1991.135

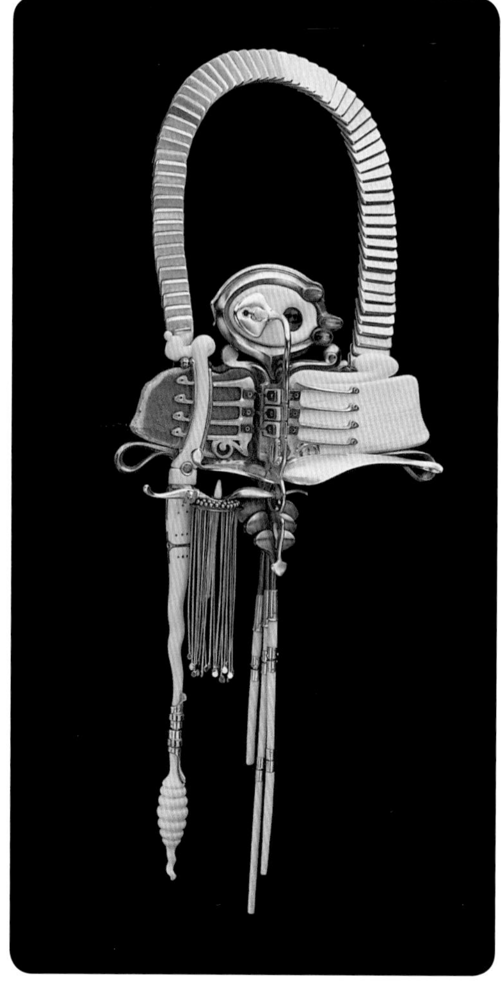

Lee A. Schuette, *Rolling Pin*, about 1975. Museum purchase, 1975.177

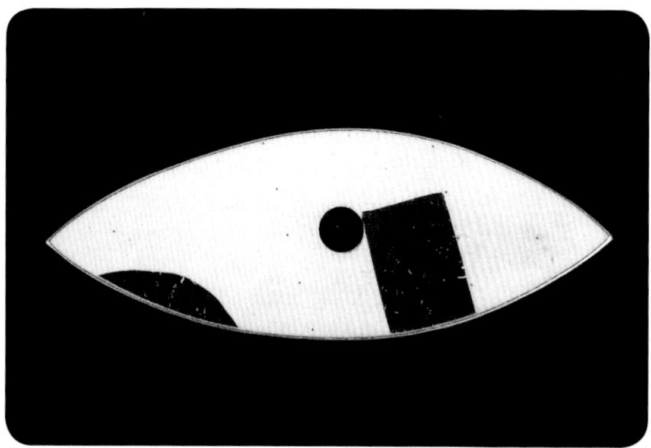

Boris Bally, *Department of Public Works Brooch*, 1994. Gift of Zack Peabody, 2000.62.2 a–c

Several artists who make furniture from metal also are represented by other objects in the collection. Before Albert Paley became famous for his large metal sculptures, he made jewelry. The Renwick Gallery is fortunate to own a pendant he created in 1973. In addition, Boris Bally fabricated metal furniture on occasion, but the Renwick collection includes a piece of his jewelry and a metal sculpture. Lee Schuette experimented with wood and metal furniture in his studio in Kittery Point, Maine, but early in has career, the museum purchased a rolling pin he had submitted to the 1975 *Craft Multiples* exhibition.

It is amazing how one chair begets many.
But each chair is designed individually.
It is a living thing.

Installation views of *The Furniture of Sam Maloof,* 2001 (above) and *Right at Home: American Studio Furniture,* 2004.

Into the New Millennium

THROUGHOUT THE ACQUISITIONS PROCESS, FURNITURE EXHIBITIONS AT THE RENWICK continued. Soon after the wicker show closed, curator Jeremy Adamson began work on the landmark Sam Maloof retrospective. *The Furniture of Sam Maloof* opened in 2001 with an accompanying catalogue of the same name. Not only was Maloof one of the best known studio furniture makers, but the Renwick owns a substantial collection of his furniture, including two versions of his signature rocker, a low back side chair, a pedestal table, a dining table, and eight chairs. Adamson's catalogue was more than a survey of the artist's career. Because Maloof began working in the 1940s, at the beginning of the studio furniture movement, and participated in most of its major events, the book presents a history of the studio furniture field.[16]

Shortly before Trapp left the museum in 2003, he selected fifty-eight objects from the eighty-two then in the collection for the 2004 exhibition *Right at Home: American Studio Furniture.* Five gems of the collection—Judy McKie's *Monkey Settee,* Sam Maloof's *Rocker,* John Cederquist's *Ghost Boy, The Rick Wrigley Renwick Cabinet,* and George Nakashima's *Conoid Bench*—were traveling as part of the *Masters of Their Craft* exhibition.[17] Even so, *Right At Home* showcased a larger number of studio furniture objects than any previous exhibition. *Right At Home* displayed even more furniture than the fifty-four pieces shown in the landmark retrospective *The Maker's Hand: American Studio Furniture, 1940–1990,* which opened at the Museum of Fine Arts, Boston at the end of 2003.[18] Although the museum did not publish a catalogue to accompany *Right at Home,* the decision was made to go forward with this present work as a comprehensive record of the entire studio furniture collection.

Today, the Renwick Gallery remains a curatorial department of the Smithsonian American Art Museum. [NMAA's name was changed to the Smithsonian American Art Museum (SAAM) in 2000.] In 2004, the Renwick implemented a new management structure. The post of curator-in-charge was abolished in favor of an administrator. Robyn Kennedy, previously an exhibition designer at SAAM, fills that position. Jane Milosch, an art historian who came from the Cedar Rapids Museum of Art in Iowa, assumed in 2005 the curatorial role vacated by Adamson in 2001. The first acquisition during their tenure was a cabinet by Jenna Goldberg, though it should be noted Trapp had done the groundwork for the addition. Since Trapp left, the Renwick has acquired one new piece of furniture, the Byrdcliffe chest.[19] The arts-and-crafts era cabinet made in the Byrdcliffe community in Woodstock, New York, entered the collection through the efforts of Heidi Nasstrom Evans, a recent James Renwick Fellow who was writing her doctoral thesis on the colony.

A new mission statement promulgated in the fall of 2005 charged the Renwick with collecting quality work by significant artists and moves away from Trapp's philosophy of collecting work by lesser-known makers. The mission statement specifies the criterion for selecting objects for the permanent collection is "the aesthetic quality of the object" and not "comprehensive coverage of the field."[20] The museum has reinstituted a program of invitational exhibitions, which were begun by Ken Trapp to exhibit work of midcareer artists. Many scholars hope the new series of exhibitions will help in the quest to acquire more work. Whatever the Renwick goes on to collect in the future, studio furniture enthusiasts are fortunate earlier curators were foresighted enough to acquire an extraordinary collection of studio furniture with both breadth and quality during the halcyon days of the movement in the last quarter of the twentieth century.

Notes

[1]Historical information about the evolution of the Renwick Gallery is based on Kenneth Trapp's essay in *Skilled Work: American Craft in the Renwick Gallery* (Washington, DC: Smithsonian Institution Press, 1998), 13–29.

[2]Trapp, *Skilled Work*, 15.

[3]The exhibition was reviewed by Joan Pearson Watkins in *Craft Horizons* 32, no. 2 (April 1972): 44–45, 68–70.

[4]Lloyd Herman, telephone conversation with the author, March 11, 2007.

[5]Miriam Davidson Plotnicov, *Craft Multiples* (Washington, DC: Smithsonian Institution Press, 1975), 15.

[6]Trapp, *Skilled Work*, 22.

[7]Davira S. Taragin, Edward S. Cooke Jr., and Joseph Giovannini, *Furniture by Wendell Castle* (New York: Hudson Hills Press, 1989), 74–79.

[8]Edward S. Cooke Jr., *New American Furniture: The Second Generation of Studio Furnituremakers* (Boston: Museum of Fine Arts, 1989).

[9]Jeremy Adamson, *American Wicker: Woven Furniture from 1850 to 1930* (New York: Rizzoli, 1993).

[10]A less quantitative and more subjective approach would be to define a work as midcareer if the artist's work continued to evolve after the piece was made. Using this criterion, all but four artists, or 94 percent, in the Renwick collection would qualify for this designation. Robert Trotman became a full-time sculptor soon after making *Louise*, and Tage Frid was forced to retire for health reasons. In the case of Evert Sodergren and Robert Whitley, when they made the pieces now in the Renwick, their work had already matured.

[11]Jenna Goldberg's cabinet was accessioned after Trapp retired, but he had initiated the acquisition.

[12]Of these, Robert Bliss, who was in his eighties, did not fit the typical profile of midcareer because he resurrected his longtime interest in furniture in 1986 after retiring from a distinguished career as an architect and professor.

[13]The Renwick collection contains multiple pieces by John Cederquist, Garry Knox Bennett, and Wendell Castle that represent both their midcareer and mature work.

[14]See pages 205 to 216 for a full statistical analysis of the Renwick Gallery's furniture collection.

[15]Kenneth Trapp, telephone interview with the author, August 2004.

[16]Jeremy Adamson, *The Furniture of Sam Maloof* (New York: W. W. Norton & Company, 2001).

[17]Kenneth R. Trapp, *Masters of Their Craft: Highlights from the Smithsonian American Art Museum* (Washington, DC: Smithsonian American Art Museum, 2003).

[18]Edward S. Cooke Jr., Gerald W. R. Ward, and Kelly H. L'Ecuyer, *The Maker's Hand: American Studio Furniture, 1940–1990* (Boston: MFA Publications, 2003).

[19]The Sodergren armchair and the Womack chest were both in the process of coming to the museum before Trapp left. The Nakashima lounge chair was transferred to the museum from the Smithsonian's National Museum of American History.

[20]Mission Statement, Renwick Gallery of the Smithsonian American Art Museum, October 19, 2005.

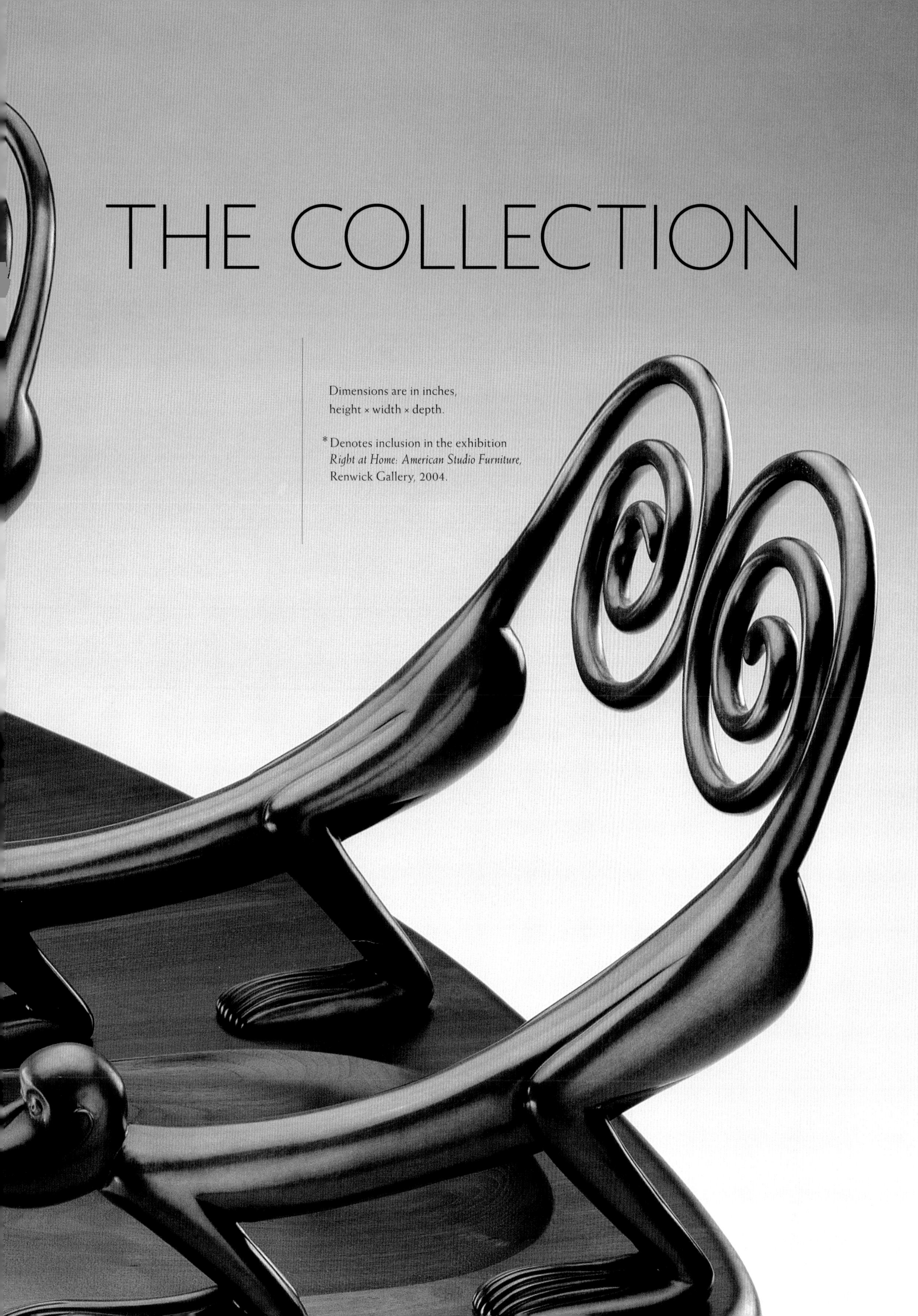

THE COLLECTION

Dimensions are in inches,
height × width × depth.

*Denotes inclusion in the exhibition *Right at Home: American Studio Furniture*, Renwick Gallery, 2004.

GARRY KNOX BENNETT

born 1934
Alameda, California

*Bench**

1979, Douglas fir, 25 ¼ × 39 ½ × 14 ⅝. Gift of Theodore Cohen in memory of his mother and her sisters, Rose Melmon Cohen, Blanche Melmon, Mary Melmon Greenberg, and Fanny Melmon Liberman, 1998.122.2a–e

ALREADY BENEFITING FROM A THRIVING JEWELRY and metal-plating business in Oakland, California, Garry Knox Bennett turned his talents in the 1970s to making metal lamps and clocks. He gradually added woodworking to his repertoire as he fabricated bases for these objects. Although Bennett is best known for his furniture that combines disparate materials such as metal, glass, and plastic, this all-wood bench is an early example of a form to which he returned repeatedly in the 1980s.[1]

Unlike most of his later work, the piece is unpainted, except for a splash of red on two of the dowels supporting the cylindrical armrests. The amorphous, cloud shapes on the ends contrast with the foursquare stance of the base. Typical of most of Bennett's work, the bench reflects his interest in form as well as his training as a sculptor at the California College of Arts and Crafts in Oakland.[2]

Bennett left the kerf marks of his favorite tool, the band saw, clearly visible on the seat, a choice confirming his dictum, "There's no labor of love here, 'cause I don't love labor."[3] He made the Renwick's bench in the same year as his famous *Nail Cabinet*, in which he drove a sixteen-penny nail into the refined padauk surface to protest the first-generation studio furniture makers' obsessions with technique and exotic woods.

[1] Information in this and subsequent catalogue entries comes largely from telephone interviews with the makers, who generously reviewed drafts for accuracy. Only Richard John and Christopher Sabin could not be located. Wharton Esherick, Tage Frid, Daniel Jackson, and George Nakashima died before the study began.

[2] California College of Arts and Crafts was renamed California College of the Arts in 2003.

[3] Ursula Ilse-Neuman, Arthur C. Danto, and Edward S. Cooke Jr., *Made in Oakland: The Furniture of Garry Knox Bennett* (New York: American Craft Museum, 2001), 65.

Preceding pages: Judy Kensley McKie, *Monkey Settee* (detail); see page 133.

GARRY KNOX BENNETT

Boston Kneehole

1989, Honduran rosewood, maple, aluminum, brick, Fountainhead, ColorCore, antiqued bronze, and watercolor, 31 ¼ × 50 ¼ × 24. Gift of Anne and Ronald Abramson, the James Renwick Alliance and museum purchase through the Smithsonian Institution Collections Acquisition Program, 1990.104

ORGANIZERS OF THE *NEW AMERICAN FURNITURE* exhibition at the Museum of Fine Arts, Boston in 1989 asked a select group of studio furniture craftsmen to choose a piece from the museum's collection and then to create a modern interpretation of it.[4] Bennett was attracted to the substantial proportions of a bureau table made in New York about 1760. As with most of his furniture, Bennett took a traditional form and fabricated it in nontraditional materials. He selected Fountainhead—a faux granite—for the top, and aluminum for the frame and a writing slide beneath the top. For the sides and the cock beading around the drawers, he used the recently developed ColorCore, a laminated plastic made by the Formica Corporation. He had used this material on a desk he submitted in 1984 for an exhibition at the Workbench Gallery in New York City and the Renwick Gallery that was organized to encourage the use of the new product.[5] In wrestling with how to treat the feet, he hit upon using solid bricks laboriously cut to conform to the contours of the façade. The drawers are rosewood, and the pulls are brass as in the original, but their linear shape contrasts with the batwing brasses on the eighteenth-century piece. Despite the disparate materials, Bennett worked them together precisely to achieve a dramatic texture across the surface.

Instead of the gentle swelling found on the façade of the original, Bennett substituted band- sawn, baroque S curves. Striations of yellow and red paint decorate the insides of the drawers and the doors underneath the top, which conceal a safe deposit box. The elegant formality of the piece may derive from the rough sketch he executed in advance, in contrast to the more spontaneous method he uses in most of his work, which he begins without much more than an idea in his head or an outline drawn directly on the wood.

---

[4] Edward S. Cooke Jr., *New American Furniture: The Second Generation of Studio Furnituremakers* (Boston: Museum of Fine Arts, 1989), 36–39.

[5] See Renwick Gallery, *Material Evidence: New Color Techniques in Handmade Furniture, an exhibition organized by the Gallery at Workbench and Formica Corporation* (Washington DC: Smithsonian Institution, 1985).

ROBERT L. BLISS

born 1921
Seattle, Washington

Deep Cradle Rocker

1992, aluminum, leather, and black Brazilian granite, 12 × 84 × 26. Gift of the artist, 1999.46.2

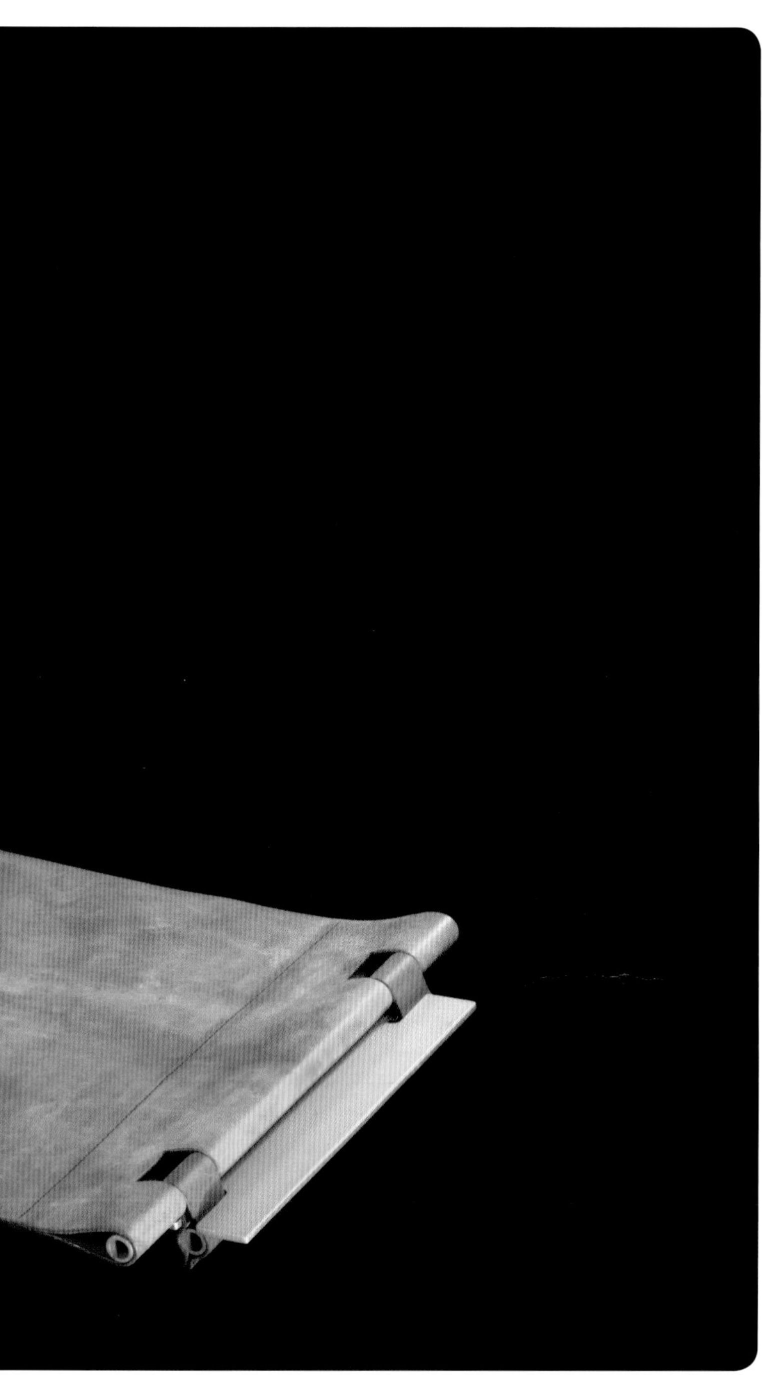

AT ONE TIME, ROBERT BLISS HAD CONSIDERED A career as a naval architect and had served in the Merchant Marine during World War II. He became interested in furniture as a student at Black Mountain College in North Carolina, where he studied under Josef Albers. He later trained with Alvar Aalto at the Massachusetts Institute of Technology, where he received a degree in architecture in 1949. After a career as a practicing architect and professor of architecture at the universities of Minnesota and Utah, Bliss retired in 1990 to pursue his interest in furniture full time in Salt Lake City, Utah.

In *Deep Cradle Rocker,* the French bridle leather, sewn by Roly Pearson, is supported on an anodized aluminum sheet that rests on a polished Brazilian granite disk. The most challenging part of the design was devising how to attach the leather to the aluminum. Bliss solved the problem by cutting slots in the aluminum sheet and attaching the leather straps to two aluminum tubes threaded through a sleeve on the top and underside of the frame. It was not unlike the solution Shinichi Miyazaki used to attach the leather to the seat of his wooden *Armchair* (see page 139). Three- and four-foot rolls of leather form two cushions, whose firmness can be adjusted by partially unrolling them. Bliss made another version of this rocker fitted with plastic mesh instead of leather. Although Le Corbusier's famous *Chaise Longue* comes to mind as an inspiration, Bliss said the idea for the rocker grew from a child's seesaw. The name for the rocker recalls the familiar words of the sea chantey "Rocked in the Cradle of the Deep."

ROBERT L. BLISS

Cradle for a Young Viking/Viqueen

1997, Baltic birch plywood and brass, 16 × 53 × 21.
Gift of the artist, 1999.46.1

BLISS'S CHILD'S CRADLE COMES IN TWO VERSIONS: one suspended from brass chain, and another set on two tetrahedrons. The Renwick's piece has both mechanisms. The polished brass tetrahedrons come apart and fold up in much the same way as Bliss's award-winning, steel Metrex display system. According to Bliss, children seem to prefer the chain version, because it swings freely. The one-eighth-inch slats of Baltic birch plywood fold together like a fan and are finished with tung oil. Like most of Bliss's furniture, the cradle is easily disassembled and packed for shipping.

The idea for the cradle came to Bliss when he was playing with strips of veneer. He saw it was possible to stack them together and put them in tension with a curved rod through the ends. After making a series of models, Bliss determined eleven strips produced the best effect. A polished brass rod, set in holes drilled at the ends of the strips and fastened with cotter pins, holds the cradle together.

Once the cradle was assembled, Bliss saw the obvious similarity to a Viking ship. Consulting with a Scandinavian friend, Bliss found there was no feminine equivalent for the word *Viking*, so he coined the term *Viqueen*.[6]

[6] Robert Bliss, telephone interview with the author, July 28, 2005.

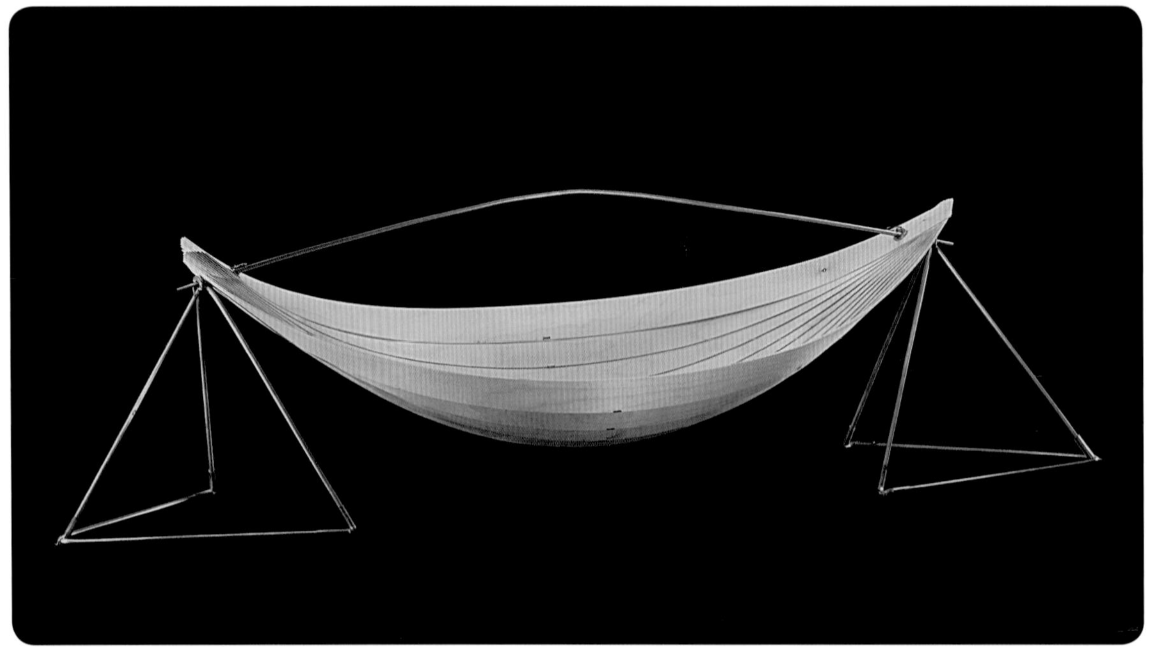

DALE BROHOLM

born 1956
St. Louis, Missouri

*Upholstered Chair**

1996, walnut burl veneer, ash, Italian poplar plywood, leather, and milk paint, 35 ½ × 28 ⅜ × 26. Gift of Marilyn and Paul O'Rourke and the Society of Arts and Crafts, 1998.114

UPHOLSTERED CHAIR GREW OUT OF A STUDENT project at Boston University's Program in Artisanry, from which Dale Broholm graduated with honors in 1984.[7] The barrel shape of the chair, made of bendable plywood, clearly reflects Broholm's interest in art deco, but the crackled surface contrasts with the refined finishes typical of the period. The soft yellow color works well with the brown leather and walnut burl. The crackle finish, which he uses often, gives the chair an aged look and a certain sparkle. Broholm made several renditions of the chair, and this one represents the final iteration. Basketball icon Michael Jordan owns two, but with a different color scheme. Since the 1990s, Broholm has begun using laser-cut inlay, and his work reflects personal ideas rather than period styles. His studio is in Wellesley, Massachusetts.

---

[7] Founded in 1975 at Boston University, the Program in Artisanry moved to the Swain School of Design in New Bedford, Massachusetts, in 1985. In 1988, it moved to Southeastern Massachusetts University in Dartmouth.

PAUL BUCKLEY

born 1951
Boston, Massachusetts

Gate-Leg Table

1975, white oak, open: 30 × 32 ¼ × 61 ¼; closed: 30 × 32 ½ × 6.
Museum purchase, 2007.14

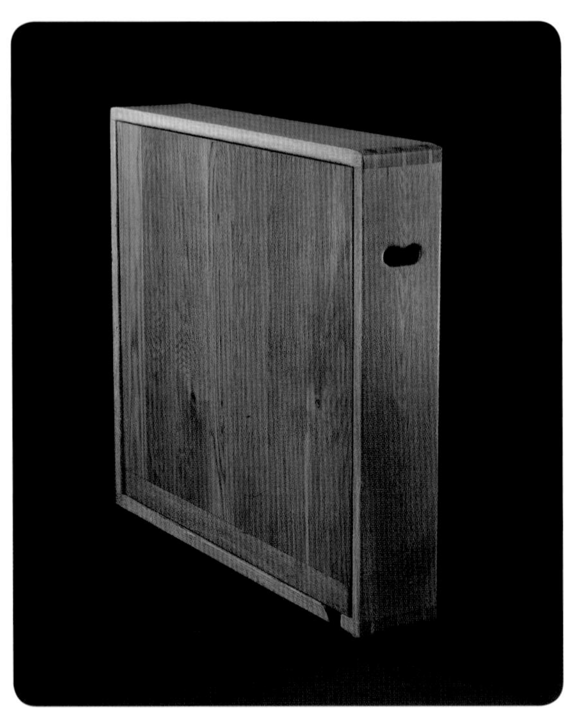

AS A STUDENT AT THE UNIVERSITY OF NEW HAMPSHIRE, Paul Buckley made *Gate-Leg Table* for a design competition sponsored by the American Woodworking Machine Institute. It won handily in the northeast region. After Buckley graduated, he entered the table in the Renwick Gallery's *Craft Multiples* exhibition in 1975. It was one of the most ingenious entries. As the saying goes, imitation is the sincerest form of flattery, but several years later Buckley was not pleased to see his design knocked-off by a national furniture manufacturer, a fate that was all too common for twentieth-century American designers.[8]

The gate-leg table tradition dates to at least the seventeenth century, when houses were small and furniture was expensive. Buckley encountered the same problems when he endured cramped student housing for four years. His modern version cleverly closes to form its own compact box. The only decorative elements in his minimalist design are carefully cut, exposed dovetails; a shaped cutout for lifting the box; and the open grain of the white oak, which he finished with oil and wax. Later versions were finished with varnish and featured tops made of edge-banded oak plywood, rather than solid wood, to give the table more stability. During his twenty-year woodworking career, Buckley made about twenty-five copies, the last for his eight-year-old daughter.

[8] Paul Buckley, telephone interview with the author, August 16, 2005.

JOHN ERIC BYERS

born 1959
Rochester, New York

*Hat Box Chest**

1999, mahogany and milk paint, 72 × 21 × 20. Gift of the James Renwick Alliance in memory of our nation's loss on September 11, 2001, 2002.2

LOOKING AT *HAT BOX CHEST*, ONE CAN EASILY IMAGINE 1950s hatboxes stacked up in the corner of a thrift shop, which, in fact, were the inspiration for this chest. John Eric Byers, who trained in the two-year woodworking program established in 1980 at the Wendell Castle School in Scottsville, New York, also acknowledged the influence of minimalist sculptor Donald Judd in his repetition of forms.

According to Byers, the chest was relatively easy to make. He mitered pieces of mahogany to form eight-sided frames, cut them round, and then stacked them eight high to form each box. The boxes were bolted together for ease of disassembly in shipping. The time was consumed in the painting process, which took as many as 150 hours—or two-thirds of the labor of making the piece. Each individual square, carved freehand into the surface, got seven coats of milk paint and was sanded between each coat to subtly expose the reddish mahogany ground. Byers's obsession with surface was reinforced during his residency with Michael Hurwitz at the University of the Arts in Philadelphia in 1986 and 1987.

The surface coloring has been compared to a Josef Albers painting, but Byers credits mosaic tiles and especially textile patterns for his inspiration. The colorful checkerboard surfaces grew out of Byers's boredom with his earlier black-painted, geometric forms.[9] The meticulously decorated, stacked, geometric cabinets have become signature works. After Byers moved from Portland, Oregon, to upstate New York in 2001, he abandoned multiple colors and now decorates his work with shades of one color. Byers admits that working the surface "can be hard on the body, but I can get really lost in it."[10]

[9] John Eric Byers, telephone interview with the author, May 12, 2004.

[10] Quoted in Deborah Weisgall, *John Eric Byers: A Mid-Career Retrospective* (Brockton, MA: |Fuller Craft Museum, 2004), 16.

CABINETMAKER UNKNOWN

Painting attributed to
Jane Byrd McCall Whitehead

Byrdcliffe Oak Chiffonier

1904, oak, stain, and oil paint, 27 ¼ × 35 × 13 ¾.
Gift of Jill and Mark Wilcox, Jr., 2005.33

IN 1903, RALPH RADCLIFFE WHITEHEAD, A WEALTHY British industrialist, moved with his wife, the former Jane Byrd McCall, to Byrdcliffe, near Woodstock, New York, where a year earlier he had founded a colony for craftsmen. Byrdcliffe furniture is rare because the total output was only about fifty pieces, most of them produced in the first year the colony was open. The furniture was costly to make, and transporting it to market in New York City proved difficult. Although the maker of this chiffonier is unknown, the panels were probably painted by Jane Byrd McCall Whitehead.[11] She was an accomplished artist who had trained in Paris and studied with John Ruskin in England. Painted on artist ply board that was inserted into the door panels, the scene probably depicts a landscape near Arcady, the couple's elaborate Tuscan-style villa near Santa Barbara, California, where they had lived since 1894. Painted panels were less common on Byrdcliffe furniture than stylized floral designs, which were carved on the majority of the furniture that was designed by Zulma Steele and Edna Walker, two former Pratt Institute students. Although some cabinets were fitted with hand-forged copper pulls made in the colony, this one has stock hardware. This chiffonier was probably built for the couple's personal use at White Pines, their home on the grounds of Byrdcliffe. This chiffonier form, based on English prototypes, was unique to the Byrdcliffe colony, which produced it in several variations.

[11] The colony employed cabinetmakers Riulf Erlandson and Fordyce Herrick and carpenters Warren Wheelock and George Eggers, any one of whom could have made this chiffonier. See Robert Edwards, "The Utopias of Ralph Radcliffe Whitehead," *The Magazine Antiques*, January 1985, 267.

ARTHUR ESPENET CARPENTER

1920 New York City
2006 Bolinas, California

*Rawhide Stool**

1972, hyedua and oak with rawhide, 27 × 15 × 15.
Gift of David L. Davies and John D. Weeden, 2001.55

ART CARPENTER GRADUATED FROM DARTMOUTH College with a degree in economics, but after visiting one of Edgar Kaufman's *Good Design* exhibitions at the Museum of Modern Art in the late 1940s, he decided to pursue a craft career. Establishing his studio in San Francisco, and later in Bolinas, California, Carpenter trained himself in woodworking. As a member of the first generation of studio furniture craftsmen, he focused on material and technique rather than design. Unlike many studio furniture makers who make one-of-a-kind objects, he was more interested in producing multiples, which he sold through his own store.

Carpenter made twenty or thirty stools of this type, with small variations. *Rawhide Stool* features three stretchers at different heights for a musician, so leg positions could be changed. While Carpenter turned legs from solid wood for many of his first stools, he shaped the legs on this example using strips of wood in the bent lamination technique. The joints are invisible because Carpenter took care to glue each quarter-inch strip back together in its original position, thus matching almost exactly the natural grain pattern.

The dark hyedua wood for the seat was imported from Ghana for use by manufacturers making hunting bows. Carpenter used hyedua often because of its strength and economical price. The underside of the seat is signed "Espenet," the maiden name of his paternal grandmother.[12] Another mark indicates that in 1993, he replaced the rawhide, which is attached by pegs on the underside of the seat.

[12] Espenet is often published as his mother's maiden name, but it was the maiden name of his father's mother. Arthur Espenet Carpenter, telephone interview with the author, April 3, 2006.

ARTHUR ESPENET CARPENTER

Band Saw Box

1972, hyedua, 8 ¾ × 16 ⅛ × 7 ¼. Gift of David L. Davies and John D. Weeden, 1998.130a–l

CARPENTER FIRST SETTLED IN SAN FRANCISCO IN 1948 and started selling turned, wooden bowls that were exhibited in the Museum of Modern Art *Good Design* shows in the early 1950s. He also taught himself cabinetmaking and began to sell furniture. Influenced notably by Sam Maloof and Wharton Esherick, his work took on an amorphous and soft-edge character that came to be characterized as the "California roundover." In addition to this box and the rawhide stool, the Renwick Gallery also owns a sixteen-foot-high staircase he produced in 1972.

This box—with eleven drawers cut out with a band saw—evolved from his experiments in the mid-1950s to make drawers without using time-consuming dovetails. He touted the virtues of this unique technique to students in the many woodworking classes he taught in the 1970s. He thought it was important to bring other people into the field and declared, "The more free spirits there are in society the better."[13] To that end he helped found the Bolinas Craft Guild, which places apprentices with various craftsmen in the San Francisco area.

[13] Quoted in Edward S. Cooke Jr., Gerald W. R. Ward, and Kelly H. L'Ecuyer, *The Maker's Hand: American Studio Furniture, 1940–1990* (Boston: MFA Publications, 2003), 114.

WENDELL CASTLE

born 1932
Emporia, Kansas

*Coffee Table**

1958, American walnut and padauk, 23 ⅜ × 63 ½ × 31. Gift of the Ruhe family in memory of Dr. Edward Lehman Ruhe, 1993.24

WENDELL CASTLE MADE *COFFEE TABLE* WHEN HE was an undergraduate studying sculpture at the University of Kansas at Lawrence, and a professor there purchased it. Always trying different approaches, Castle wanted to support the tabletop without using the traditional four legs. The padauk top is held between organic supports shaped in walnut that rise from the floor and reach over the edge to clamp down on the top from above. The wood is finished with linseed oil.

Although the table's shaped edge recalls the irregular wooden slabs George Nakashima cut for surfaces of his furniture, Castle had never heard of Nakashima at that point in his young career. Castle carefully cut out the top, not to show off the grain of the wood as did Nakashima, but to produce a pleasing, abstract, sculptural form. Working in a sculpture studio, he had few woodworking tools other than a band saw. After earning his bachelor of fine arts degree in 1958, the same year he completed this table, Castle stayed at the University of Kansas to pursue a master's degree in industrial design. Although he has devoted most of his career to one-of-a-kind objects, he has occasionally dabbled in limited production work, such as his plastic "Molar" group for Stendig and Beylerian in the early 1970s and, more recently, a line for Holly Hunt.

WENDELL CASTLE

*Music Stand**

1975, walnut, 42 ⅛ × 26 ⅜ × 19 ¼. Museum purchase, 1975.168

CASTLE SUBMITTED *MUSIC STAND* FOR INCLUSION in the *Craft Multiples* exhibition at the Renwick Gallery in 1975. It was among sixty-four objects purchased by the museum to travel around the country. The three legs are clamped and glued over a form in the bent lamination technique and then joined to the base with a long scarf joint. The organic shape of the stand and the oiled walnut are reminiscent of Danish modern furniture popular in the 1950s and 1960s. Although not a musician himself, Castle had some musician friends, so it seemed natural to make the form at that time in his career. Castle subsequently made about a dozen music stands in his shop in Scottsville, New York.

WENDELL CASTLE

*Ghost Clock**

1985, Honduran mahogany, 86¼ × 24½ × 15. Museum purchase through the Smithsonian Institution Collections Acquisition Program, 1989.68

AFTER HIS TECHNICAL SUCCESS WITH TROMPE L'OEIL work in the 1970s, Castle, at the suggestion of New York gallery owner Alexander Milliken, turned his attention to more conceptual work. Originally planning to make twelve clocks for the *Masterpieces of Time* exhibition, Castle decided to add a thirteenth, totally nonfunctional piece as a surprise addition and as the culmination of his trompe l'oeil oeuvre.

The last and most significant piece in that series, *Ghost Clock*—modeled after a sheet-draped, eighteenth-century tall case clock he borrowed from a local antique dealer—was carved from a massive, laminated block of wood.[14] To replicate the linen sheet, Castle repeatedly bleached the mahogany, but left the grain raised to simulate the texture of the material. Even today, gallery visitors, fooled by the ingeniously effective trompe l'oeil, wonder why the sheet has not been removed.

Purposefully tying the sheet at the waist of the clock with meticulously carved string, Castle wanted to impart an anthropomorphic quality to the "grandfather" clock and instill a sense of curiosity about what lies under the sheet. The Milliken Gallery wrote that the clock "symbolizes the end of time, the ethereal and mysterious afterlife that no human can decipher—or unwrap."[15]

[14] This artwork was originally titled *Ghost*. However, over time the piece has become known as *Ghost Clock*.

[15] Quoted from an undated note from Alexander Milliken in the Renwick Gallery's artist file.

WENDELL CASTLE

*Desk with Clock 2**

1991, coachwood, mahogany, patinated bronze, and leather, 37 ½ × 54 × 21. Gift of Peter T. Joseph, 1998.34.1

WHEN IS A DESK NOT A DESK? CASTLE DESIGNED THIS desk to disguise its use. Where did the idea come from? Castle declared, "Anything I see, hear, or read may invade my work. I probably misinterpret all of this information."[16]

The focal point of the desk is the clock with a bright bronze face, unmarred by numbers, perched on the canted top surface. Two giant, patinated, bronze legs cradle the desk section. The severe rectilinearity of the wooden desk contrasts with the amorphous shape of the cast bronze legs. The only hint a desk is present is the thin, bronze handle with which to raise the top and expose the writing surface. Three pockets in the lid and two drawers below the writing surface provide storage for papers and other office supplies.

Castle's genius lies in his ability to reinvent himself. Comparing this desk to his earlier coffee table (see pages 52–53), it is hard to imagine they are made by the same hand. Yet, he has pursued a kind of consistency as well. Wharton Esherick showed Castle that furniture could also be regarded as sculpture. Throughout Castle's illustrious forty-year career, the overriding theme of his work has been an emphasis on sculptural qualities.

[16] Michael Hosaluk, *Scratching the Surface: Art and Content in Contemporary Wood* (Madison, WI: Guild Publishing, 2002), 94.

JOHN CEDERQUIST

born 1946
Altadena, California

*Storage Drawers and Mirror**

about 1975, imbuia, leather, mirror, and brass, 37 ¾ × 19 ⅝ × 10 ⅝.
Museum purchase, 1975.169.

IT SEEMS IMPOSSIBLE THAT THIS MIRRORED WALL cabinet was created by John Cederquist, since he is best known for his Japanese-inspired trompe l'oeil work. Its rounded art deco façade was influenced by the anthropomorphic, sculptural shapes Wendell Castle was creating about the time Cederquist graduated from California State University at Long Beach with a master's degree in craft. The leather, more commonly used for prostheses, is shaped over a form and sewn with a prominent edge reminiscent of the standing metal seam on the roof of a vintage Bugati automobile. *Storage Drawers and Mirror* was displayed in the *Craft Multiples* exhibition at the Renwick in 1975 and purchased by the museum after the show.

JOHN CEDERQUIST

Kimono to Go

1991, plywood, veneers, epoxy resin, gold leaf, and aniline dye, 78 × 38 × 15. Gift of MCI, 2001.89.32

CEDERQUIST WENT OUT TO BUY BENT PLYWOOD AND returned with three half-cylinders he thought might make nice drink cabinets. He made *Wannabe* and *Little Wave* with two of them, and the third cabinet became the start of the "Kimono" series. The size of the semicircular tube determined the scale of the cabinet, and he based the design on a *kosode* (literally, short sleeve) he had seen exhibited in London in the 1970s.

Precursors of the modern kimono, the bright textiles are considered national treasures in Japan. Although woven in the seventeenth century, *kosode* relate more closely to modern design than to textiles in Old World Europe, where they were virtually unknown. The gold leaf medallions that represent Japanese clan signs usually appear on sleeves and backs of kimonos, but following the pattern on the kimono that inspired this one, Cederquist scattered them across the surface with abandon.

As is typical with his work, Cederquist plays with perspective in his rendering of the box from which the kimono emerges (hence the title). Usually, he is concerned his compositions make visual sense at least from a single point, but in this example the perspective is modified so the composition is not a true illusion, much in the manner of the fantasies in an M.C. Escher print.

Another exhibition at the Los Angeles County Museum of Art in 1992 entitled *When Art Became Fashion: Kosode in Edo-Period Japan* led to a series of eleven additional kimono cabinets. Instead of a realistic rendering of the elegant Japanese textiles as on *Kimono to Go*, Cederquist fancifully decorated these later cabinets with giant carp, falling leaves, stylized ocean waves, Popeye cartoons, vintage aircraft, and even Mickey Mouse.[17] Tired of working on the big, cumbersome and difficult-to-make cabinets, Cederquist has recently turned to more manageable objects, like a series of trompe l'oeil trays.

[17] See Franklin Parrasch, *John Cederquist: Kosode Built as in a Dream* (New York: Franklin Parrasch Gallery, 2005).

JOHN CEDERQUIST

Ghost Boy

1992, birch plywood, sitka spruce, and poplar with copper leaf, epoxy resin inlay, and aniline dyes, 88 ¼ × 44 ½ × 15. Gift of the James Renwick Alliance, Ronald and Anne Abramson, and museum purchase, 1993.51

FOR THE LANDMARK *NEW AMERICAN FURNITURE* exhibition at the Museum of Fine Arts, Boston in 1989, Cederquist chose to reference a high chest of drawers made by John Townsend in Newport, Rhode Island, about 1760. Cederquist entitled his interpretation of that piece *Le Fleuron Manquant* (The Missing Finial) in memory of a finial lost when the museum loaned the high chest to another museum.[18] *Ghost Boy,* made three years later, is a variation on the theme. Here, the finial is found and prominently displayed in its rightful place on the pediment. A white pickle stain imparts a deathly pallor to the high chest, hence the name *Ghost Boy,* a takeoff on the modern term *highboy.*

Adapting techniques from Japanese woodblock printmaking and American cartoons, Cederquist executed the design using inlay, epoxy resin, and lithography ink. In *Le Fleuron Manquant,* the piece seems to be taken apart and packed in crates for reassembly. *Ghost Boy,* too, has that effect, and when one looks carefully at the parts, it is clear they have been distorted and broken up so they would not fit back together, much like a cubist painting. The crates themselves look roughly assembled from scrap wood, in contrast to the finely worked wood used to make the eighteenth-century masterpiece.

Both Cederquist pieces function as chests, although the placement of the parallelogram-shaped drawers bears little relationship to the trompe l'oeil façade. Further disorienting the viewer, Cederquist renders his designs so they can be viewed realistically from only a single point. As the viewer moves around the pieces, the perspective becomes distorted. Through distortion, Cederquist plays with the viewer's sense of reality and takes the surrealist concepts of René Magritte and others to another level. Magritte had to remind viewers, "This is not a pipe" in his famous 1929 painting of a pipe, which he called *The Treachery of Images* or *The Treason of Images.* Cederquist's cabinets do not appear to be cabinets, but they really are.

[18] Cooke, *New American Furniture*, 40–43.

JOHN CEDERQUIST

*Chaise Marlin**

1999, Baltic birch plywood, gum, maple, poplar, epoxy resin inlay, and aniline dye, 46 × 70 × 38. Gift of the James Renwick Alliance, 2000.7

AS A NATIVE CALIFORNIAN WITH A SHOP IN SAN Clemente, Cederquist is influenced by things Japanese and the sea. The two ideas commingle in *Chaise Marlin,* one of two related benches that is a technically challenging departure from his more common cabinets. A stuffed marlin Cederquist saw mounted on a wall was the direct inspiration, but he also remembered seeing cartoons of marlins swimming around with bent bills. The trompe l'oeil wooden boards over the eyes form an *X* to symbolize the death of the fish. The *X* is a reminder of the time a friend caught a marlin on his boat, and when they saw it staring up at them, they were moved to release it out of sympathy.[19]

Appearing on a number of his pieces, the Japanese characters on the crest of this bench loosely translate as "conserve," meaning conserve the marlin or conserve nature in general. The five characters on one leg of the bench represent Cederquist's initials. The rope, a new motif for him, has no real significance beyond the visual function of tying the piece together. He first used the shipping crate image, which forms the structure of the bench, in a 1989 cabinet that appeared to be constructed of shipping crates, and again in *Le Fleuron Manquant* (The Missing Finial), the highboy for the *New American Furniture* exhibition of that year.

[19] John Cederquist, telephone interview with the author, April 3, 2006.

DAVE CHAPMAN

born 1968
Bay Village, Ohio

*Couch**

1994, willow and aspen, 31 × 60 × 36. Gift of Shelby and Frederick Gans in honor of Elizabeth Broun, director of the Smithsonian American Art Museum, 1998.26

THE TRADITION OF MAKING FURNITURE FROM WILLOW was introduced into the United States by immigrant gypsies (Roma) from Eastern Europe. In 1992, Dave Chapman learned the craft from Clifton Montieth, one of the pioneers in the field, while attending the University of Michigan at Ann Arbor, where he received a bachelor of fine arts degree. Willow attracted Chapman because it was elastic like clay, with which he had worked in college. Yet in willow he could build larger, more complex pieces. He also experimented with wood but found it too restrictive, and it required a prohibitively expensive workshop for the budget of a recent graduate. All that was needed for willow work was a drill, hammer, Japanese saw, and garden clippers.

After graduation, Chapman lived with Montieth and his wife in northern Michigan, helping them renovate their farmhouse and build a new studio. At the same time, he created a body of work that would in 1994 become part of his first one-man show at the Revolution Gallery in Royal Oak, Michigan. *Couch* was part of that show. Originally, Chapman planned to fit the couch with rockers to mirror the curve of the crest rail, but he decided he liked the billowy, transparent lightness of the overall form he grounded on solid legs.

In 1996, Chapman moved to California, where he opened his own studio in San Francisco. He cut his own willow from creek beds and streams outside the city, and then cleaned, sorted, and bent the willow to create chairs and sculptures.[20] Before driving each nail to assemble the piece, he drilled a hole to avoid splitting the wood. Then as the wood dried, it shrank around the nail to hold it tight.

Chapman's work is all about defining inside and outside space. He enjoys the discovery process and never knows exactly how a project will turn out. Natural variations in the willow influence the developing shape and often inspire him to detour from his original design.[21]

[20] Dave Chapman, telephone interview with the author, April 2004.

[21] Ibid.

STEPHEN COURTNEY

born 1953
Oceanside, New York

*Secretarial Desk**

1998, maple, copper leaf, copper-plated cast bronze, glass, leather, and golf tees, 43 × 48 × 25. Gift of the Mortenson Family Foundation, LLC, Madison, Wisconsin, 2003.54

A SELF-TAUGHT ARTIST, STEPHEN COURTNEY SUPPORTS his passion for creating modern interpretations of classic furniture with a thriving cabinetmaking business in Los Angeles. He found inspiration for this desk in a photograph that a girlfriend gave him depicting an arts-and-crafts style desk with a fold-down writing surface. In his work, he experiments with form and shape rather than ornament. *Secretarial Desk* reflects his preference for combining unlikely materials and imparting a sense of humor to make his pieces less intimidating.

Courtney chose golf tees to fill the curved glass top because of their texture and because they were made of maple, which is one theme of the desk. (See detail page 6.) The shape of the legs suggests golf tees, too, but it was accidental. Actually, the balls at the top of the legs are the exact diameter of softballs, a reference to his favorite sport. The hammered copper front recalls a pile of maple leaves turned brown in the late fall. The lid folds down to reveal a pair of Doric columns, behind which rows of spindles form cubbyholes. The spindles echo the sticklike legs and the golf tees on the exterior. Courtney displayed *Secretarial Desk* at the second annual Furniture Society meeting at the California College of Arts and Crafts (now the California College of the Arts) in Oakland, where Kenneth Trapp, the keynote speaker, saw it and acquired it for the Renwick's collection.

JACOB CRESS

born 1944
Norton, Virgina

Oops! *

2001, mahogany, 40 × 20 × 18. Gift of the artist, 2002.53a–b

A FORMER NAVY SAILOR, SOMETIME ACTOR, AND self-trained cabinetmaker, Jacob Cress began repairing and reproducing Chippendale and country furniture in 1974. About ten years later, he started making "nontraditional" furniture as a change of pace from his reproduction business in Fincastle, Virginia. These projects enable him to poke fun at cabinetmakers who take themselves too seriously, much in the same vein as Garry Knox Bennett's 1979 *Nail Cabinet*.

Oops!, number nine in a series of ten, depicts an eighteenth-century Philadelphia Chippendale chair that has released the ball from its claw and is frantically trying to recapture it. Cress used the same theme for his *Oops!* table, but with less success because it lacks the anthropomorphic qualities of the chair, an effect heightened by the painted eyeballs attached to the splat. Slightly oversized, the ornately carved chair contains hardly a straight line, making it the most difficult piece he produces, requiring more than 150 hours to fabricate.

PETER DANKO

born 1949
Washington, D.C.

*Molded Plywood Chair (prototype)**

1978, maple and fabric, 31 × 20 ⅛ × 24 ⅛. Gift of Lloyd E. Herman, founding director and director emeritus of the Renwick Gallery (1971–1986), in honor of Michael W. Monroe, curator-in-charge, Renwick Gallery (1986–1995), upon the occasion of his retirement, 1995.83

THE IDEA FOR A ONE-PIECE PLYWOOD SEAT WAS NOT new, but Peter Danko's chair was the first practical one to be mass produced. In 1874, Isaac I. Cole of Hillsdale, New Jersey, received a patent for a bent plywood chair, and in the 1930s, Finnish architect Alvar Aalto continued those experiments. In England, Gerald Summers produced the first chair made from a single piece of plywood in 1933, but it was not widely distributed. The front legs were fragile and tended to break with use.[22]

After a 1976 visit to the Thonet factory in Statesville, North Carolina, Danko was inspired to try his hand at bentwood furniture. He solved the durability problem by using ten thin sheets of wood stacked with the grain running in alternating directions. He glued and pressed them together under 150 tons of pressure. The trick was to apply just the right amount of heat at the thickest points so the glue would set properly. To simplify construction, the prototype was made in two-and-a-half-inch-wide strips and then glued and doweled together, unlike the production models that were made from a single sheet of plywood. The prototype was one-of-a-kind, but the production model, which has evolved into the more curvaceous *Body Form* chair, is still produced by Persing Enterprises in Red Lion, Pennsylvania.

[22] David A. Hanks, *Innovative Furniture in America from 1800 to the Present* (New York: Horizon Press, 1981), 73.

PETER DANKO

*Unfolding Chairs**

about 1981, maple plywood, 31 ½ × 19 ¾ × 19 ¾ each.
Gift of Joseph N. Raffa, 1997.119.1–2

AFTER GRADUATING FROM THE UNIVERSITY OF Maryland with a bachelor's degree in fine arts in 1971, Danko began his career making furniture on commission. He soon migrated to production design because it offered him more control over the design process. With commission work, he explained, "You kind of end up doing what the customer wants to do."[23]

Most folding chairs are made of metal to address the need for storable furniture, but Danko's *Unfolding Chair* was an elegant solution in wood. After repeated experimentation he discovered, much to his surprise, that the curve that provides the most comfort for the seat is the same curve that most comfortably supports the back. The thickness of the plywood varies according to structural needs. The nylon hinges, which Danko developed with a National Endowment for the Arts design fellowship, are molded into the plywood. The custom-made clips are nylon coated so that the chair will close easily. The chairs came in red and black as well as natural. Danko produced these chairs in his own factory in Clinton, Maryland, for only a short time between 1981 and 1985. Although he considers them among his best designs, they could not compete with the cheap metal ones that cost one-tenth as much.

[23] Cooke, Ward, and L'Ecuyer, *The Maker's Hand*, 116.

PETER DANKO

Harry's Desk

1982, walnut, white oak, and leather, 28 ¾ × 77 × 43 ⅞.
Gift of Harry K. Schwartz, 1997.13

BEFORE PETER DANKO BECAME INTERESTED IN ECO-modernism and limited production, he completed a number of one-of-a-kind commissions. He made this desk in his shop in Clinton, Maryland, for Harry Schwartz, a Washington D.C., lawyer, who gave Danko free rein to do whatever he wanted. He liked the challenge of desk design but rarely had the opportunity to build such complex commissions.

The paisley shape of the top, repeated in the base, relates to a desk Danko saw in the Museum of Modern Art in New York City by turn-of-the-century French art nouveau architect and designer Hector Guimard. The diagonal termination of the base, which supports the cantilevered top, was suggested by a similar configuration on the Guimard desk as well as related diagonal vectors so prominent in the work of Gerrit Rietveld, a leader of the Dutch de Stijl movement in the early twentieth century. A chair by Richard Riemerschmid, a German designer and architect, displayed with the Guimard desk also featured the diagonal vectors. Additionally, Danko acknowledged the influence of biomorphic, cantilevered executive desks by Wendell Castle.

To shape the base, Danko clamped and glued thin sheets of white oak over a form, in contrast to his later work that was formed in hydraulic presses. Dark walnut—used for the kick plates, stiles, and top—frames the white oak façade. As a result, the base seems to float magically in space. A final, elegant detail is the pullout, leather-covered writing slide with four fitted drawers beneath. He finished the oak with lacquer and coated the black walnut with a special mixture of linseed oil, turpentine, and polyurethane. According to Danko, when he told his friend Sam Maloof about the formula, it became Maloof's favorite finish for his own work.

JOHN DUNNIGAN

born 1950
Providence, Rhode Island

*Slipper Chairs**

1990, purpleheart with silk upholstery, 26 ¾ × 26 ½ × 23; 43 ½ × 26 ¼ × 24.
Gift of the James Renwick Alliance, 1995.52.1–2

ALTHOUGH JOHN DUNNIGAN STUDIED UNDER TAGE Frid as a graduate student at the Rhode Island School of Design, it was a classics professor who introduced him to historic design. Inspired by eighteenth-century slipper chairs, Dunnigan's interpretations are low to the ground and are intended for perching, not lounging. The over-sized seats emphasize a key part of a chair, while the narrow backs are understated. The mass of the seats contrasts with the delicacy of the backs, creating an interesting proportional tension.

In the 1980s, Dunnigan collaborated with Wendy Wahl, a textile designer who would later become his wife. For *Slipper Chairs,* however, Dunnigan chose a Mark Pollack fabric to evoke a luxurious, eighteenth-century French feel. Wahl provided the tassels on the crest rails. Originally standing straight up on the taller chair, the tassels suggested Dunnigan's graying hair. The tassels lie over the rail like pigtails on the shorter chair and, together with the splash of purpleheart, refer to Dunnigan's wife and her red hair. Unique interpretations of tassels and their unorthodox placement were a signature element in his work during the 1980s and 1990s. Dunnigan thought tassels were sexy and provocative, and claimed they were "not something expected from a white male woodworker."[24] His shop is in West Kingston, Rhode Island.

[24] John Dunnigan, telephone interview with the author, May 2004.

DAVID EBNER

born 1945
Buffalo, New York

Stool

1974, black walnut, 16 ½ × 15 ⅞ × 14 ⅛.
Museum purchase, 1975.170

DAVID EBNER STUDIED WITH WENDELL CASTLE AND Bill Keyser at the Rochester Institute of Technology in the late 1960s and spent two years at the London School of Furniture Design. When the Renwick Gallery first opened in the early 1970s, Ebner was serving in the U.S. Army and stationed in the Washington, D.C., area. He immediately submitted an entry when he saw the announcement for the *Craft Multiples* show in 1975. He had worked out the stool design using a pine prototype before he constructed this example in black walnut. The shape, reflecting his interest in Japanese design, suggests a *torii,* the post-and-lintel gateway to a Shinto temple. Fabrication involved a combination of fine joinery for the hand-cut dovetails, and sculpting and shaping the seat and uprights with a variety of tools, including spokeshaves, rasps, and pneumatic sanders. Ebner finished his early stools with linseed oil but now rubs on a high-grade tung oil, often used for gunstocks, and then applies a final coat of lacquer. Working in his studio in Bellport, New York, he invests about thirty hours in making each one.

Ebner had originally given this stool to his mother, but she returned it saying it was too nice. Along with his *Scallion Coat Rack* (shaped like a giant scallion), this design has become one of his signature pieces. Over the years, Ebner has produced thirty or forty of them in a number of different woods. Purpleheart is the most popular. As a result of collaboration with folk artist Ivan Barnett in the mid-1990s, he began casting the stools in bronze.

Several years after the Renwick show, Washington, D.C., collector Ronald Abramson commissioned a two-seater version of the stool for an exhibition in the Museum of Fine Arts, Boston. Both one- and two-seater variations are, says Ebner, "approachable" and easy to use as either seats or side tables.[25]

[25] David Ebner, telephone conversation with the author, April 21, 2004.

ROBERT ERICKSON

born 1947
Lincoln, Nebraska

Floating Back Rocker

2000, fiddleback maple, 46 ⅝ × 32 ¾ × 42 ⅜.
Gift of Martha Drexler Lynn and Robert Danzinger, 2000.54

ABOUT NINETY PERCENT OF ROBERT ERICKSON'S work consists of chairs, which are, according to his customers, the most comfortable custom-made chairs in the studio furniture field. In the late 1970s he began custom fitting his chairs to each client. Unlike Sam Maloof, who uses his own body as a template, Erickson takes several body measurements and then, after watching the way customers sit in his chairs, he makes up to a dozen adjustments to the seat, crest rail, and arm height to fit the individual. The curve of the back varies depending upon the style of chair. In the case of *Floating Back Rocker* for Robert Danzinger, however, he misread the measurements for an earlier chair he had made for the client, and it turned out too narrow. Consequently, the Danzingers graciously offered to donate the chair to the Renwick.

Erickson calls it a *Floating Back Rocker* because the slats fit loosely into the mortises cut in the crest rail and the seat, an idea he developed in 1975 after seeing a similar technique used by Elam Sharpe, an elderly wheelwright from northern California. For the next eight years, he improved on the technique. In 1983, Erickson took it one step further by laminating the slats and shaping them into curves that would support the lower back. Since then his technique has been copied by a number of craftsmen. By varying the thickness of the slats, he can adjust the flex of the back.

Erickson's work shows the influence of Danish designer Hans Wegner, whose furniture he saw firsthand on a trip to Denmark. Erickson was particularly struck by the Dane's attention to fine craftsmanship, even on the unseen surfaces. He also was impressed with the amount of detail Sam Maloof put into the hand-shaping of his furniture, a process that would be difficult to mass produce. Maloof's influence also is apparent in the arrises on the arms of his rocker, but the rest of the frame is more rounded than that of a typical Maloof-designed chair. Tullen Eugene Bach did the sanding and finishing of this piece, and his initials appear on the underside of the seat along with the name Bodie Wagner, Erickson's longtime shop assistant in his studio in Nevada City, California.

Before becoming interested in woodworking, Erickson pursued a pre-dentistry program for two years then changed to an English major. After college, he moved to the San Francisco area and apprenticed with Ed Stiles and Roger Somers, who showed him the way to make a living in the studio furniture field. Inspired by wood and iron farm tools, knives, and ice axes, his latest work incorporates iron and aluminum with wood.

WHARTON ESHERICK

1887 Philadelphia, Pennsylvania
1970 Paoli, Pennsylvania

*Desk**

1950, cherry and walnut, 29 ⅞ × 62 ¾ × 32 ¾.
Gift of Robert B. Frank, 1977.69

THE PATRIARCH OF THE STUDIO FURNITURE MOVEMENT, Wharton Esherick influenced several first-generation makers such as Sam Maloof and Art Carpenter. Esherick's organic, sculptural designs inspired many in the second generation as well, including Wendell Castle, Dan Jackson, Jere Osgood, and David Ebner. Castle spoke for numerous colleagues when he said, "Esherick taught me that the making of furniture could be a form of sculpture."[26]

Indeed, it was Esherick's furniture displayed at the 1939–1940 New York World's Fair that first brought studio furniture to a wide audience. He had collaborated with architect George Howe to furnish the America at Home Pavilion with a dining room table and four chairs. The Renwick Gallery recognized Esherick's importance by including him in their 1972 inaugural exhibition *Woodenworks*.

Desk, like his studio in Paoli, Pennsylvania, has no straight lines, probably a reaction to the razor-straight edges on art deco furniture that was so popular when he began his career. His edges are rolled over, and the sides are curved, a design that complicated the construction of the exposed dovetails joining the top to the sides. Like the dovetails by James Krenov, another member of the first generation of studio furniture makers, these are irregular, with twenty-one across one edge and twenty-three on the opposite edge.

Esherick studied sculpture at the Pennsylvania Museum and School of Industrial Art (now called the University of the Arts) and the Pennsylvania Academy of the Fine Arts. As a cabinetmaker, Esherick was self trained and contracted the construction of most of his furniture to his neighbor John Schmidt. Esherick initially experimented with exotic woods such as padauk but eventually decided he could work just as well with locally available woods like walnut and cherry.

[26] Sam Maloof and Wendell Castle, "Wharton Esherick 1887–1970," *Craft Horizons* 30, no. 4 (August 1970): 11.

MAXIMILIAN RAINER FACKLAM

born 1960
Düsseldorf, Germany

*Travel Vanity and Stool**

1997, ebony, ash burl veneer, pearwood, aluminum, silk, and leather; vanity with travel case: 45 5⁄16 × 20 5⁄8 × 16; stool: 20 ½ × 11 3⁄16 × 11 7⁄8. Gift of an anonymous donor, 1998.53a–c

TRAINED IN SCULPTURE, PAINTING, AND ART HISTORY in the Kunstakademie in Düsseldorf, Germany, Rainer Facklam also studied at the Art Students League in New York City, where he now resides. His *Travel Vanity and Stool* reflect his continuing interest in elegant boxes and containers made with rare woods and metal common in the art deco era.

Facklam fitted the vanity with three storage drawers in front, faced them with ash burl veneers featuring a highly complex grain pattern, and added a pop-up mirror and sliding tray on either side for use at home. The aluminum travel case, packed with an assortment of seventy-eight cosmetics and accessories, stands ready for immediate use on the most exotic of trips. Designed for the jet set, the case is fitted with only the most stylish brands, such as Chanel makeup, a Louis Vuitton address book, French perfumes, and a Mont Blanc pen. Adding a sense of adventure to the contents are a wine stopper, corkscrew, pair of napkins, and six votive candles. Made in a limited edition of ten, each travel case is custom fitted to meet the needs of individual owners.

DOUGLAS PAUL FINKEL

born 1963
New York City

*Source Bench**

1999, painted poplar and rope, 17 ½ × 27 × 12.
Gift of Marcia and Harry Thalhimer, 1999.103

DOUGLAS FINKEL RECEIVED HIS MASTER'S DEGREE from the School for American Crafts at the Rochester Institute of Technology and now teaches in the Studio Furniture/Wood Program at Virginia Commonwealth University, which was founded in 1968 in Richmond, Virginia. First experimenting with this bench form in graduate school, he based the design on African headrests initially discovered by art deco designers such as Pierre Legrain in the early twentieth century. The curved seat also recalls traditional Japanese *torii* temple portals, which influenced Sori Yanagi's *Butterfly Stool* from the 1950s, as well as David Ebner's *Stool* (see page 82) from the 1970s.

The manila rope wrapping the seat adds color and texture to the surface, which Finkel painted black and then sponged over with red paint. The chisel cuts on the base are laid out in a regular pattern using a jig, and the seat is textured by hammering the soft poplar. Finkel coopered each half of the base, joining together nine pieces of wood cut to compound tapers. He has made about thirty-six of these benches using different woods, textures, and materials—some covered with Kinte cloth, others with bleached, scorched, or natural wood. He considered this variation his most successful.

RICHARD FORD

born 1966
Middleboro, Massachusetts

*Uncle Rick's Wonderland**

1997, painted poplar with mirror, 72 × 22 × 72.
Gift of Leo Kaplan Modern, 2000.103

RICHARD FORD GREW UP IN NEW ENGLAND SURROUNDED by American antiques. He received his bachelor of fine arts degree in furniture design at the Swain School of Design in New Bedford, Massachusetts, and then went on to earn his master's degree in 1995 under Wendy Maruyama in the furniture program at San Diego State University. Ford's furniture designs started with traditional Chippendale forms, which he then animated and exaggerated. In *Uncle Rick's Wonderland,* the tripod supports flanking the case suggest eighteenth-century tea tables, while the mirror recalls rococo dressing glasses. The case is fashioned from two sheets of bendable plywood clamped over a form, but other elements are roughed out with a band saw and then finished using an auto-body grinder.

Ford enjoyed the finishing process the most, even though it consumed half of the time required to make the piece. He applied more than twenty coats of acrylic paint mixed with water-based lacquer to achieve the rich surface appearance. He dubbed the process, "Fordachromed," and explained, "Color and surface design are the 'icing on the cake' of my exaggerated forms."[27]

Ford's three-year-old relative gave this piece its title. When asked if his creation looked like something out of *Alice in Wonderland,* the child replied, "No. It looks like Uncle Rick's wonderland." (Rick is the artist's nickname.) The title stuck.[28] The Renwick's piece is one of three, all of which vary in color and detail. Ford liked using furniture as a medium for his art because of its wide appeal. For the same reason, he added a cartoon quality to reach a broader audience. Despite his success in the studio furniture field, he decided several years ago to close his shop in Maryland and pursue a business career.

[27] Hosaluk, *Scratching the Surface,* 89.

[28] Richard Ford, telephone interview with the author, May 2004.

PAUL FREUNDT

born 1951
Savannah, Georgia

*Troas**

1999, patinated bronze, 35 × 24 ½ × 22 ⅛.
Gift of Douglas E. Macon, 2000.80

PAUL FREUNDT EARNED HIS MASTER OF FINE ARTS (MFA) degree in sculpture at Georgia State University in Atlanta, and several of his public sculptures dot the landscape in that city. After twenty years of working in Atlanta, he moved his workshop to Talking Rock in the mountains of north Georgia in 1995. His recent interest gravitates toward tables and chairs. *Troas,* which is the ancient name for Troy and is a nod to the classical origins of metal furniture, typifies his minimalist, abstract works that are surprisingly comfortable.

The tubular legs play against the sharp edges of the triangular seat and back. Inspired by primitive art and work from the Bronze Age, Freundt applied multiple layers of patina that, together with heating and grinding, give this chair a light bronze color. For *Troas* he reversed the normal configuration of three-legged stools by putting the single leg in front and the two legs at the rear.

TAGE FRID

1915 Copenhagen, Denmark
2004 Newport, Rhode Island

*Three Three-Legged Stools**

1982–83, walnut, 30 ¼ × 20 × 15 ½; 26 ⅜ × 17 ⅞ × 12 ⅝; 21 ¼× 16 × 11.
Museum purchase, 1988.8.1–3

TAGE FRID WAS A GIANT IN THE FIELD OF STUDIO furniture. Trained in his native Denmark, he was lured to America in 1948 to head the School for American Craftsmen at Alfred University, which began offering the first four-year degree in craft in the country. The program moved to the Rochester Institute of Technology in 1950. Frid left that program in 1962 to chair the Department of Furniture at the Rhode Island School of Design, where he taught until he retired in 1985. In addition to teaching, Frid wrote books on furniture craftsmanship and articles in *Fine Woodworking* magazine, of which he was a founder. In all of these endeavors as well as his studio works, Frid influenced three generations of furniture makers.

The stools in the Renwick collection demonstrate his core belief that construction techniques should determine design. While sitting on a fence rail to watch a horse show, Frid realized that a large seat was not necessary. In these examples, the six-inch-wide seats gently taper, becoming thicker in the middle where the single rear leg enters the seat. He repeated the flattened oval form of the seats in the handhold on the crest. He first attached plain turned legs to the stools and let them sit in his studio for a few months before finally realizing what they needed. Frid decided that turned, tapered legs would complete the design.

JENNA GOLDBERG

born 1968
Brewster, New York

Falling Leaves

2004, painted basswood, 75 ⅝ × 24 ¼ × 16. Gift of Cantor Judith Bender in memory of Dr. Michael and Leona Bender, 2005.7

BASED IN PROVIDENCE, RHODE ISLAND, JENNA Goldberg works mostly on commission, so she relished the opportunity to explore her own personal preferences in this cabinet, which was two months in the making. Trained as an illustrator, she sees her cabinetry as canvas to decorate with subjects drawn from nature, particularly as interpreted on Japanese textiles. She responds to their bold colors and the sparseness of their stylized designs. "Japanese design is what it is," she says, "simple but sophisticated at the same time."[29] She paints the outside of her cabinets freehand using a carefully laid out grid system. The difficulty of wrapping a grid around a curved surface explains the rectangular shape of most of her case pieces.

Goldberg fashions the proportions of the case for a taller-than-average person, but she also has to be able to get it out the studio door. The black base serves as a proper pedestal for the exterior composition. The purposeful irregularity of her carving, which outlines the leaves and flowers, mitigates the effects of the rigid regularity of the surface pattern. Although Goldberg earned her bachelor's degree from the University of the Arts in Philadelphia and her MFA from the Rhode Island School of Design, Goldberg learned carving from Kristina Madsen. Goldberg thinks of it as a link with her earlier life as an illustrator, where she used a pencil to outline her drawing. Carving serves as a bridge between her two-dimensional painting and the three-dimensional cabinet.

Her favorite colors of Japanese red and black that decorate the eye-popping, stylized leaves on the outside of the cabinet contrast with the surprisingly soft yellows of the more subdued cranes on the inside. (See inside detail, page 204.) Besides the difference in colors from outside to inside, the techniques differ as well. The interior was decorated before final assembly using special rubber stamps in the manner of Japanese woodblock printing or handmade wallpaper. When using the stamping technique, softer colors give better detail than dark ones.

Falling Leaves contains another surprise on the interior: vertical slats cover the back where a solid sheet of plywood would be expected. The slats subtly suggest an old kitchen cabinet interior covered with layers of paint or contact paper or the typical wall covering of a Victorian summer cottage that she would like to own someday. It is natural to compare Goldberg's work to that of Judy Kensley McKie (see page 132), who also was trained as an artist. Goldberg's work is always full of decorative surprises and delicious whiffs of the past that stir the viewer's imagination just as vividly as McKie's mysterious animals.

[29] Jenna Goldberg, telephone interview with the author, September 2005.

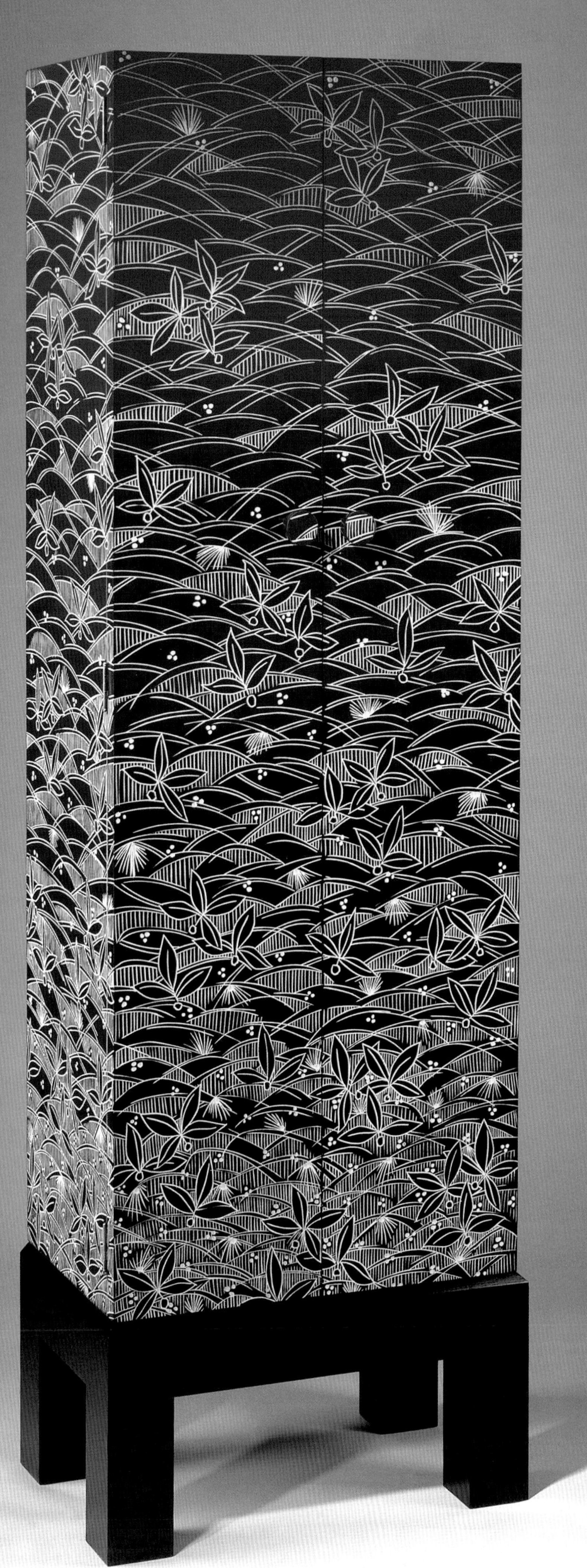

JOHN HIGGINBOTHAM

born 1962
Greensboro, North Carolina

Curly Maple Corner Chair

1999, East Coast curly maple with aniline stain and lacquer finish; damask upholstery (with padded horsehair slip seat), 31 × 24 × 24. Gift of John and Marie Higginbotham, 2000.22

LOOKING FOR FEEDBACK ON HIS WORK, JOHN Higginbotham entered a mahogany corner chair in the 2000 *Chair Show 3* exhibition in Asheville, North Carolina. Serving as one of the jurors, Kenneth Trapp encouraged him to submit a similar one in maple for possible acquisition by the Renwick. Working in a guitar factory on Maryland's eastern shore, Higginbotham was familiar with the difficulties of working with maple because of its irregular grain pattern. For the most challenging task of shaping the crest rail, he was forced to use a scraper rather than a chisel because the latter tore out too much wood. The effort was worth it; the effect is like a gentle cresting wave.

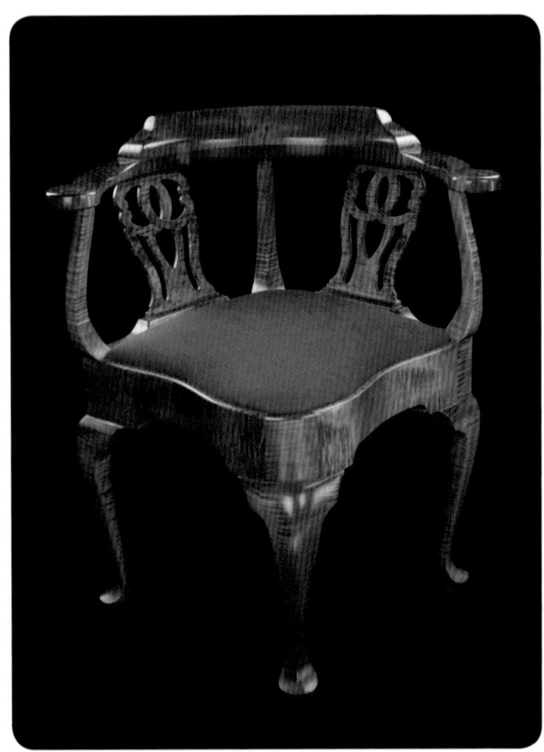

Lovingly producing the prototype for his wife, Higginbotham has since made a half dozen of these corner chairs. The legs and arms are sawn out of a solid plank as mirror images of each other and then shaped. In contrast to eighteenth-century practice wherein the entire pad foot is lathe-turned, he turned only the thin disk on the bottom of each foot and shaped the rest of the leg by hand. The slip seat rests in rabbet joints cut into the two front rails and on two rosewood strips screwed to the two back rails. In order for the splats to meet the generous arc of the crest rail, Higginbotham had to angle them sharply. The splats are carved from a solid piece of wood in the eighteenth-century manner to suggest interlacing strapwork vaguely reminiscent of Boston Chippendale chairs.

As with most of his work, this corner chair is a conscious blending of several eighteenth-century designs. The compressed splats and the generous proportions are designed to accommodate his own body and reveal a modern sensibility. Although influenced by the arts-and-crafts movement's love of wood, the selection of highly figured maple appeals to a twentieth-century aesthetic. Only if mahogany were not available or was deemed too costly would an eighteenth-century customer opt for locally grown maple—and even then it was generally stained to make it look as much like mahogany as possible. Higginbotham has applied an aniline stain, but only to heighten the delicious, honey color of the maple, not to imitate mahogany.

THOMAS HUCKER

born 1955
Bryn Mawr, Pennsylvania

Low Table

**1985, Brazilian beefwood, bronze, and waxed linen string, 15 ½ × 85 ½ × 20 ½.
Gift of Bebe Pritam Johnson, Warren Eames Johnson and Peter T. Joseph,
1991.131a–c**

THOMAS HUCKER SET UP A STUDIO IN JERSEY CITY, New Jersey, after graduating from the Program in Artisanry (PIA) at Boston University in 1980. Two years later, he submitted this design for the *Please Be Seated* exhibition at the Museum of Fine Arts, Boston. Although he had intended this piece to serve as a table, he thought it would work equally well as a bench. A study in proportion and linear form, *Low Table* makes obvious reference to bridges and to Japanese design. He developed an appreciation for the Japanese aesthetic while attending the Urasenke School of Tea Ceremony in Boston.

The top is set into keys that protrude above the surface, drawing the eye to the subtly curved support rails. The top is attached to the rails with linen thread through brass buttons, so that the top can move slightly as the wood expands and contracts. The dark beefwood from Brazil, similar to, yet harder than, mahogany, contrasts with the polished bronze supports. He contracts out the bronze casting, specifying a dark or light patina depending upon the choice of wood. He learned his careful attention to technique mostly from Sam Maloof during a summer at the Penland School of Crafts in North Carolina and from Jere Osgood, his teacher at PIA. This table is his most popular piece, and he has made more than a dozen since creating the first one in the early 1980s.

MICHAEL HURWITZ

born 1955
Miami, Florida

*Rocking Chaise**

1989, mahogany, steel pipe, and milk paint, 36 × 90 × 24. Gift of Anne and Ronald Abramson, the James Renwick Alliance, and museum purchase made possible by the Smithsonian Institution Collections Acquisition Program, 1990.102

A VISIT TO THE RENWICK GALLERY IN 1972 TO VIEW *Woodenworks* introduced Michael Hurwitz to the studio furniture field. After an early interest in making musical instruments, Hurwitz graduated from Boston University's Program in Artisanry with a strong sense of the historical sources for furniture. His work also reflects his travel to Japan and the Dominican Republic.

Rocking Chaise was made for the *New American Furniture* exhibition at the Museum of Fine Arts, Boston in 1989.[30] Always interested in light construction, Hurwitz was drawn to an early nineteenth-century Boston side chair by Samuel Gragg in the museum collection. He took Gragg's innovative bentwood design and essentially tried to turn it into a magic carpet. Prominent, raised dovetails at the base of the chaise pay homage to similar joints that attach the slats to the seat frame in Gragg's chair.

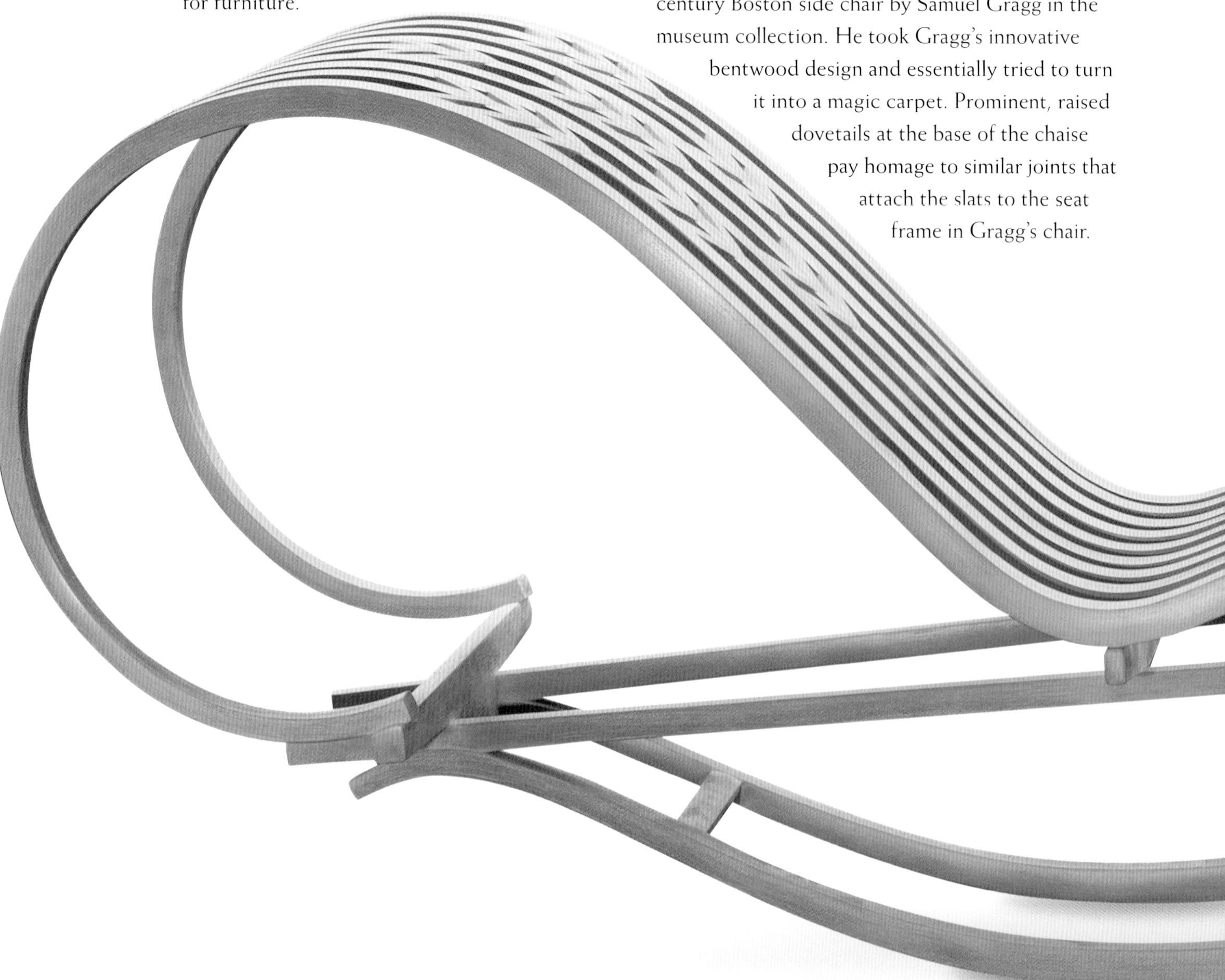

Although the chevrons at the head of the chaise recall stylized trees or peacock feathers that were painted on the original Gragg chair, the reason Hurwitz gives for including them was simply to provide more mass to the surface. The structure of the base suggests typical Japanese house construction. Too light to safely support the chaise, the base is reinforced with two horizontal metal rails encased in wood. The week before the exhibition opened, he refinished this piece, replacing a glazed, oil-based finish with a milk paint surface.

Working in Philadelphia, Hurwitz has made a number of variations of this chaise and recently has experimented with furniture that incorporates labor-intensive mosaics and a variety of other materials including stone, raw Indian silk, slate, Damascus steel, papyrus, and salvaged glass. Confirming his interest in surface, he has experimented with some favorite finishes, including milk paint with its variegated shades of color; oil enamel, which he sometimes mixes with marble dust to create texture; gouache, which has rich and saturated color; and cashew, which looks like traditional Japanese lacquer, but lacks its poisonous component.[31]

---

[30] Cooke, *New American Furniture*, 60–63.

[31] Jonathan Binzen, "Michael Hurwitz: Furnituremaker's Gift," *Woodwork*, no. 97 (February 2006): 24–31.

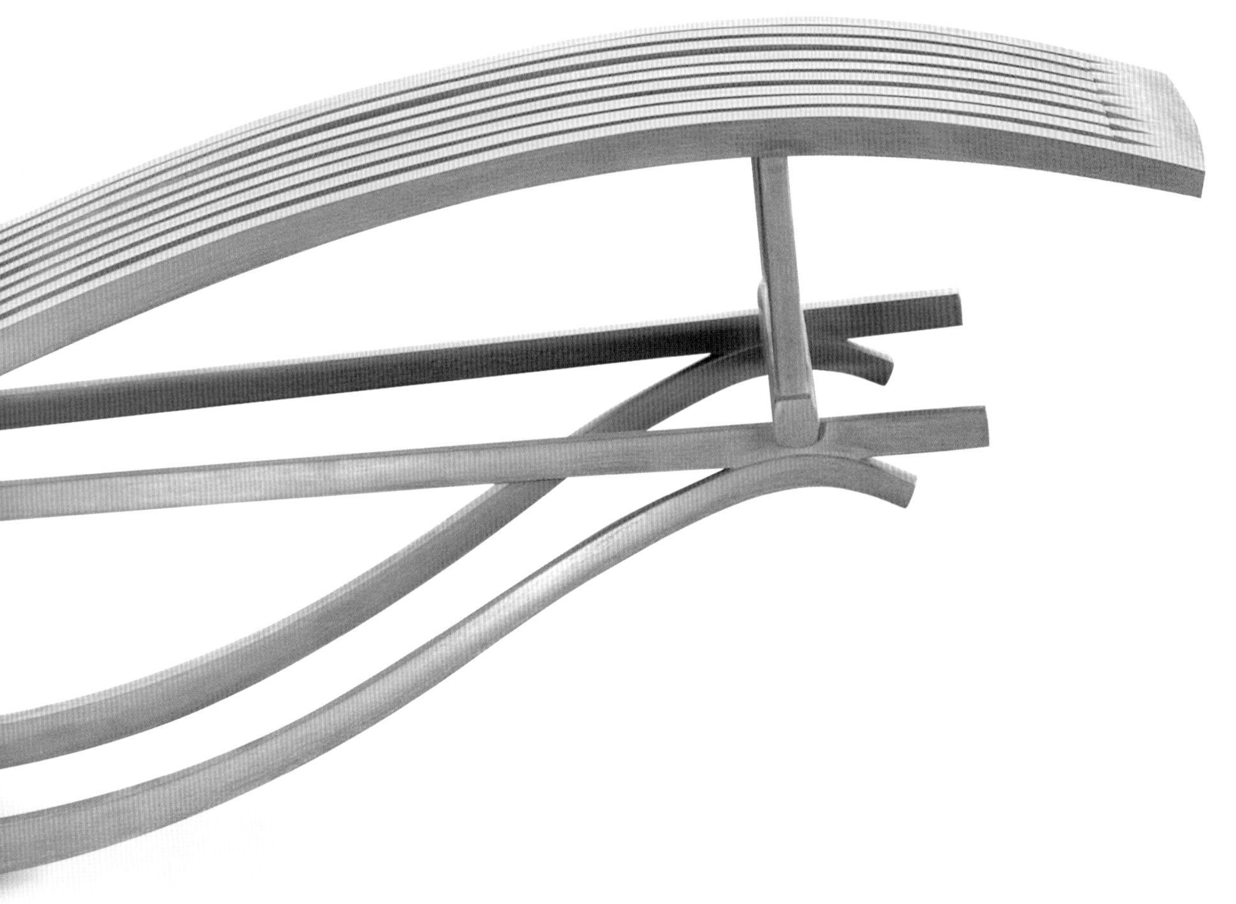

DANIEL JACKSON

1938 Milwaukee, Wisconsin
1995 Milwaukee, Wisconsin

*Four Step Library Ladder**

1965, black walnut and oak, 78 ½ × 20 ½ × 25 ¾. Gift of the James Renwick Alliance and museum purchase made possible by the Smithsonian Institution Collections Acquisition Program, 1990.54

DANIEL JACKSON'S MOTHER WAS AN ANTIQUE DEALER in Wisconsin, and he was buying and restoring antiques by the age of thirteen. Totally immersed in the Scandinavian approach to design, he studied under Tage Frid at the Rochester Institute of Technology and then enjoyed a two-year apprenticeship with Peder Moos in Denmark. Serving as a bridge between the first and second generation of studio furniture makers, Jackson founded the Philadelphia College of Art wood program in 1964, and in 1975, was a founding member of the Program in Artisanry at Boston University.[32] His influence is apparent in the free-spirited work of his students, who included Alphonse Mattia, Ed Zucca, James Schriber, and Thomas Hucker. Unfortunately, a debilitating illness in 1976 left Jackson unable to work and cut short his promising career.

The library steps reflect his grounding in the Danish cabinetmaking tradition, even down to the rounded mortises cut by a horizontal boring machine he had first seen in Peder Moos's shop in Denmark. These steps give no hint of the playfulness of Jackson's later work, epitomized by such pieces as *Rocking Peacock*, which is the size of a merry-go-round horse.

[32] The Philadelphia College of Art, founded in 1876, merged with the Philadelphia College of Performing Arts in 1987 and was renamed the University of the Arts. It was led in the 1980s by Michael Hurwitz, Peter Pierobon, and Richard Kagan, and later by Roy Superior and Jack Larimore. See *The Maker's Hand*, which contains brief histories of all of the major schools that offer training in furniture making.

RICHARD R. JOHN

born 1948

*Music Rack**

1975, black walnut and ebony, 44 × 19 ½ × 12 ¾.
Museum purchase, 1975.171

WHILE A HIGH SCHOOL STUDENT IN VIRGINIA, Richard John won a scholarship from the Fisher Body division of General Motors for an automobile design. He went on to study engineering at Virginia Polytechnic Institute in Blacksburg and then transferred to the Art Center College of Design in Los Angeles. He later worked for the industrial design firm of Henry Dreyfuss Associates in New York before returning to California to pursue a full-time career in furniture making.

Music Rack was accepted for the Renwick's *Craft Multiples* show in 1975. Following the lead of the patriarch of the studio furniture movement, Wharton Esherick, most furniture makers felt the need to experiment with music stands at some point in their careers. The cut-out ebony forms that support the sheet music suggest hammers used to play a xylophone or perhaps a series of notes from a musical score.

TOM LOESER

born 1956
Boston, Massachusetts

*Four by Four**

1994, mahogany with acrylic and milk paint, 44 ¼ × 33 ¾ × 17. Gift of Robert and Gayle Greenhill, Eleanor T. and Samuel J. Rosenfeld, anonymous contributors, and museum purchase, 1995.92

TOM LOESER HAS BUILT MANY CABINETS AND CHESTS with multiple drawers, but in most of them, he manipulated the drawers or used tricky mechanisms. This cabinet, part of a series of three, is primarily about structure, using color to bring out the geometry of the piece. Even the title, *Four by Four,* emphasizes the number of drawers and the drawer configuration. Influenced by the Memphis Group and by Alphonse Mattia at the Program in Artisanry, from which he graduated in 1982, Loeser has been a pioneer in the use of paint on wood since the early 1980s. Since 1991, he has headed the University of Wisconsin at Madison's woodworking and furniture design program, which was founded by Skip Johnson in 1965. Some of Loeser's most recent furniture incorporates a kinetic dimension.

In *Four by Four,* he applied thirty-four different colors of milk paint to decorate the surface. Each drawer front received two unique colors, either from the yellow/orange family or the blue/purple family. The finish coat was sanded with fine steel wool, both to polish the surface and to expose a little of the red mahogany on the edge of the fluting to introduce yet another color. The composition relates to Josef Albers and his ideas about working with contrasting colors. A former faculty member of the German Bauhaus, Albers taught color theory at Yale University, where he chaired the design department.

Preferring handwork to power tools when possible, Loeser used a gouge to cut the fluting on the drawer fronts but resorted to a grinder to make the larger cuts on the sides of the case. "I like painting on the thin edge," says Loeser, "and the definition that the edge then gives to the larger planar surfaces."[33] The drawer dividers overlap in a woven pattern to knit the piece together visually. Even more important than providing visual mass at the base, the flared feet create a critical sense of tension with the rigid checkerboard grid on the façade.

[33] Cooke, *New American Furniture*, 66.

DANIEL MACK

born 1947
Rochester, New York

*Eel Gig Chair**

1992, maple and found objects, 56 × 21 × 21. Gift of Frederick Wiedman Jr. in memory of Richard Mack, 1999.33

FORMERLY A JOURNALIST, DANIEL MACK TAUGHT himself to make furniture, ultimately deciding he could more effectively communicate through his furniture than through writing. The rustic tradition in furniture goes back at least to the tenth century, when the Chinese made furniture out of tree roots. It was revived in the eighteenth century to feed the appetite for the exotic and was practiced by the gypsies (Roma) in Eastern Europe and the Celts in Ireland. By the nineteenth century, rustic furniture appeared in English gardens and soon arrived in American parks. Frederick Law Olmsted installed rustic furniture in Central Park in New York City, and it was a short step from there to New Yorkers' summer camps in the Adirondacks.

The *Eel Gig Chair* is part of Mack's "Memory" series, chairs made with branches and found objects that include woodworking tools, oars, and fishing tackle. The eel gigs in this chair have an unambiguous use to stab eels, but here they are pointing up in a less threatening position. It is impossible not to recall Grant Wood's famous painting *American Gothic*, featuring the farmer with the pitchfork. The fishhook, strategically placed at the center of the back, symbolically snags the viewer. Mack lives in Warwick, New York.

KRISTINA MADSEN

born 1955
Northampton, Massachusetts

*Dining Chair**

**1993, imbuia, silk, and metal, 33 × 20 ½ × 18 ½.
Gift of the James Renwick Alliance, 1998.82**

KRISTINA MADSEN DEVELOPED AN EARLY INTEREST in quilting, weaving, sewing, and lacemaking, but in the 1970s, she trained to be a cabinetmaker by working with Englishman David Powell at the Leeds Design Workshop in Easthampton, Massachusetts. Powell along with John Tierney, an administrator from Boston University's Program in Artisanry, had founded the Leeds Design Workshop in 1977. Until it closed in 1989, the program enrolled up to twenty-one students in a two-year traditional joinery curriculum.

In the mid-1980s, Madsen began to incorporate intricate patterns, done with a router, into her work. These designs were based on Fijian and Maori examples that she had seen in a catalogue of Pacific artifacts. While serving as an artist-in-residence in Australia in 1988, she visited numerous exhibitions of Oceanic objects that deepened her interest in carved surfaces. In the early 1990s, Madsen returned again to the South Pacific and studied with Fijian carvers. Giving up the router that she used earlier, she now executes new carving patterns, evolved from these South Pacific traditions, entirely by hand.

For this chair, Madsen chose imbuia, a South American wood similar to walnut, because it has a consistent grain and takes a stain well. She stained it black like Fijian carvings, so the design will catch the light. "It is this light, the reflected light, the bouncing light, that I love," she explained.[34] A red silk Jack Lenor Larsen upholstery fabric creates a dramatic contrast with the black surface. The shape of the splat, which is carved on both front and back, is based on the shape of a Hawaiian fan. She used three tools to do the carving—a gouge for the circular cuts and sixty- and ninety-degree parting tools for the angular cuts. The parting tools make the V cut, suggesting a shark's tooth, a common Fijian motif. She executes the carving freehand, making small adjustments to ensure her designs fit the given space.

Every piece has a different pattern. Madsen carved this chair as a sample for a client who wanted a set of six. After the client opted for an uncarved set, the chair was purchased for the museum with funds from the James Renwick Alliance. Early in her career, Madsen specialized in chairs, but since the 1990s, she has concentrated on benches and case pieces that provide a larger canvas for her carving. Madsen's studio is located in Southampton, Massachusetts.

[34] Michael Goodison, ed., *Sit Up and Take Notice! A Gathering of Artist Benches* (Northampton, MA: Smith College Museum of Art, 2003). See essay about Kristina Madsen.

SAM MALOOF

born 1916
Chino, California

*Drop-leaf Dining Table with Wood Hinges and Eight Texas Dining Chairs**

1975, Brazilian rosewood and leather, table: 28 × 44 ¼ × 110; chairs: 38 × 21 ½ × 21 each. Gift of Blanche Pope in memory of Edker Pope, 2001.82a–i

STILL WORKING IN HIS NINETIES, SAM MALOOF IS among the best known of the first generation of studio craftsmen. Along with Wendell Castle, John Cederquist, and Garry Knox Bennett, Maloof is one of a handful of studio furniture makers who have been the subject of solo exhibitions in major museums. He is the only furniture maker to receive a MacArthur Fellowship. A self-trained cabinet-maker, he worked for three years for Millard Owen Sheets, a well-known California artist, before becoming a full-time cabinetmaker in 1949.

In 1973, Mr. and Mrs. Edker Pope visited Maloof's workshop and showroom in Alta Loma, California, and left an order for a rocking chair. Hours later the Popes called Maloof to ask for forty-three pieces of rosewood furniture to fill their seaside home in Corona del Mar, California. It took about a year to complete the order, which included this table and eight *Texas Chairs.* Although Maloof liked the grain and color of rosewood, he was allergic to the dust.

In the early 1960s, he had developed the *Texas Chair,* characterized by the low arms and the horn-like crest rail suggesting a Texas longhorn steer. Maloof touted the advantages of the low arm that "acts as a handle, and, structurally, takes the place of a stretcher below the chair seat."[35] He shaped the crest rail with the new Surform rasp introduced by Stanley in 1960. The table takes a traditional trestle form, but with the addition of two drop leaves on the ends. Maloof produced the tabletop by gluing thirteen strips of wood the same width as the wooden hinges that hold the leaves. A concealed brass rod holds the hinges together.

[35] Jeremy Adamson, *The Furniture of Sam Maloof* (New York and Washington, DC: W. W. Norton and Company in association with the Smithsonian American Art Museum, 2001), 97. The information for all the Maloof entries comes largely from this excellent catalogue.

SAM MALOOF

Rocker

1980, walnut, 44 ¾ × 45 ¾ × 26 ¾.
Gift of Roger and Frances Kennedy, 1997.88

WOODWORKERS GENERALLY AGREE ROCKING CHAIRS present the most difficult technical challenge of any furniture form. Although the rocking chair would become Maloof's signature piece, he produced few of them before the 1980s. He made his first rocking chair for his wife, Freda, in 1958, but it was not until 1961, after he received a note from Henry Dreyfuss, the well-known industrial designer and one of Maloof's clients, that he began to design rocking chairs in earnest. The note enclosed a clipping from the *Wall Street Journal* reporting the sale of rockers was taking off after President John F. Kennedy's physician touted the relaxing benefits of rocking.

Maloof's rockers from the 1960s typically had upholstered seats, turned spindles on straight backs, stretchers, and a crest rail that extended past the back posts ending in hornlike projections. By 1975, the evolving rocker design substituted flat, curved spindles for the straight, turned ones; featured a crest rail contained within the stiles; and replaced the upholstered seat with a shaped wooden one. *Rocker* also incorporated the special slotted dado-rabbet joint, developed in 1974, which allowed Maloof to eliminate the stretchers. Compared with the Renwick's walnut rocker, typical of production during the 1970s and 1980s, his chairs of the 1990s feature more curves, thinner headrests, and showier maple.

In the Renwick's example, the underside of the seat is incised "no. 20 1980/Sam Maloof F. A.C.C./made for/Roger Kennedy SAM MALOOF." He used the F. A.C.C. notation for seventeen years after he was selected as a Fellow in the American Craft Council in 1975. In 1992, he changed the marking to d.f.a.r.i.s.d. to commemorate the honorary doctorate of fine arts he received from the Rhode Island School of Design that year.[36]

[36] Adamson, *The Furniture of Sam Maloof.*

SAM MALOOF

*Pedestal Table**

1992, fiddleback maple, 21 ¾ × 23 ⅝ diam.
Gift of Sam and Alfreda Maloof, 1992.105

MALOOF IS AT HIS FINEST MAKING CHAIRS. HIS TABLES, which of necessity require wide flat surfaces, do not have the same tactile and sculptural quality he imparts to his seating furniture. The organically shaped legs of this table suggest tree roots, but they lack the subtle curves of his chair legs.

SAM MALOOF

*Double Rocking Chair**

1992, fiddleback maple and ebony, 42 ⅝ × 42 × 44 ½. Gift of the Hafif Family Foundation, the James Renwick Alliance, and museum purchase made possible by the Smithsonian Institution Collections Acquisition Program, 1992.115

MALOOF INTRODUCED A DOUBLE VERSION OF HIS rocker in 1987 and has made more than a dozen since then, including one for his friends, former U.S. President Jimmy Carter and his wife, former First Lady Rosalynn Carter. The carefully chosen, highly figured fiddleback maple is accented with ebony plugs and strips inserted into the bent laminated rockers. The distinctively curved, flat spindles in the back evolved from a request by a customer in the early 1970s for a chair that would give her good lumbar support. Like most of his chairs since the 1970s, *Double Rocking Chair* has what he called "hard edges" to heighten its tactile and sculptural quality. As with all of his designs, Maloof used his own body as a template to perfect the right curve.

SAM MALOOF

*Low-Back Side Chair**

1995, ziricote, 29 ¾ × 22 ¾ × 22 ⅛. Gift of Alfreda and Sam Maloof in honor of Michael W. Monroe, curator-in-charge, Renwick Gallery (1986–1995), 1995.29

MALOOF, WITH HELP FROM HIS TEENAGE SON SLIMEN, made the first version of the low-back side chair in 1966 for Mrs. J. Burgen Evan of Northfield, Illinois. As it evolved over the next thirty years, it became one of Maloof's favorite designs. The original featured the rounded edges typical of his early Scandinavian-influenced work and an upholstered seat found on most of his chairs until the 1970s. *Low-Back Side Chair* shows the "hard edges" and refined shapes that typify his later furniture. Maloof even made a settee form of the chair, first with an upholstered seat and central leg supports and later with a wooden seat and no central legs. The brown ziricote wood, native to Mexico and Central America, has characteristic black streaks running through it.

ALPHONSE MATTIA

born 1947
Philadelphia, Pennsylvania

*Points of Reference: Atlas, Webster, & Roget**

1995, Baltic birch plywood and various hardwoods with glass and gold leaf, a: 72 × 19 × 13 ½; b: 70 × 21 ½ × 15 ½; c: 66 ½ × 19 × 18. Gift of Peter T. Joseph, 1998.34.2a–o

ALPHONSE MATTIA ENJOYS TELLING STORIES. A frustrated filmmaker and writer, he uses furniture as a way to narrate his ideas about life. He has been one of the pioneers in freeing studio furniture from the obsession with material and technique. Mattia once declared, "When I first started using paints it was a mild sort of rebellion from what I saw as the tyranny of the woodiness of wood."[37] He studied with Dan Jackson at the Philadelphia College of Art and then with Tage Frid at the Rhode Island School of Design, where he earned his master of fine arts degree. Mattia went on to teach in the Program in Artisanry at Boston University with Jere Osgood and now works at the Rhode Island School of Design, where his wife, Rosanne Somerson, heads the furniture design program.

Mattia likes to start with familiar objects as a way of capturing his audience. In the early 1980s, he gained national attention with his series of Hans Wegner-inspired, anthropomorphic clothes valets that conveyed both serious and humorous messages. His series of "Step Vanities" refer to his childhood memories of the basement steps where his father used to store things as sort of a family archives. The reference book idea grew out of an earlier work called *Slang Dictionary,* a stand that he made in conjunction with the publication of the *Dictionary of Slang* published by Random House.

In making the Renwick piece, Mattia was reminded of the authority invested in books by a Woody Allen skit.[38] While standing in line for a movie, Allen argues with the man ahead of him about Marshall McLuhan's theory that electronic communications have defined our age. He turns around and there is McLuhan himself, so Allen asks McLuhan to settle the disagreement. McLuhan tells him to consult his book, *Understanding Media: The Extensions of Man.* In the skit, as in life, books not only settle arguments, but they preserve and transfer knowledge. They help create a cohesive culture with shared information. Acknowledging the social value of reference books in particular, Mattia included three in *Points of Reference.* The significance of a dictionary and atlas is evident. A shared understanding of words and places is crucial to effective communication. But Mattia needed a third book, so he chose *Roget's Thesarus,* even though he did not consider it as essential as the other two.

[37] Hosaluk, *Scratching the Surface*, 72.

[38] Alphonse Mattia, telephone interview with the author, May 10, 2004.

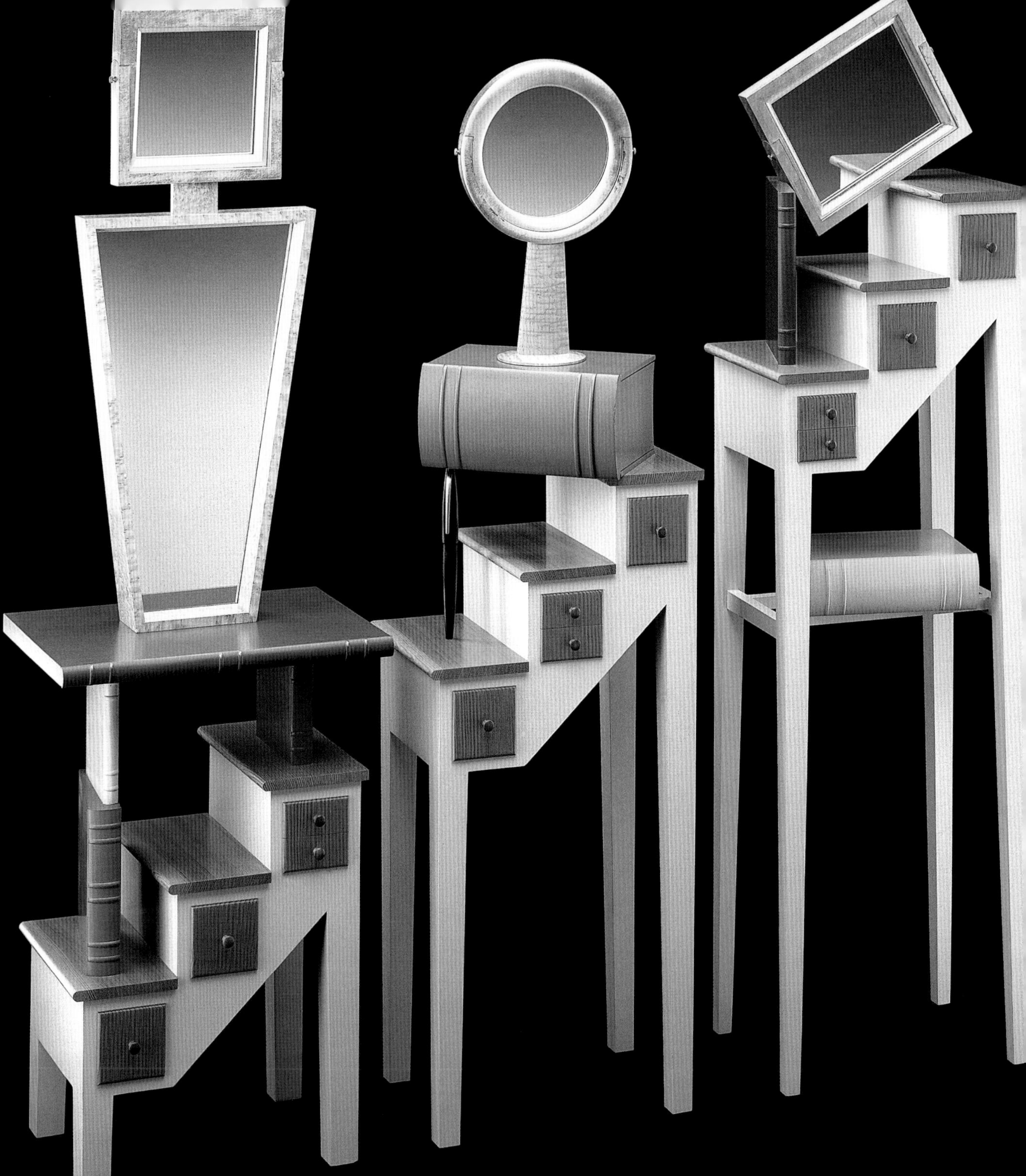

RORY MCCARTHY

born 1948
New York City

*Dining Table**

1976, padauk, wenge, imbuia, bubinga, shedua, glass, Plexiglas, and aluminum, 40 ¾ × 77 ¾ diam. Gift of Walter Rich, 1991.167

WHEN RORY MCCARTHY STARTED OUT IN THE EARLY 1970s as a self-taught cabinetmaker in Tucson, Arizona, his furniture, with all of its compound curves and sensual features, reminded people of the work of Antonio Gaudi, the art nouveau architect in Barcelona, Spain. When McCarthy looked at Gaudi's furniture, he realized they were right, so he went in a different direction.

This table combines mechanistic gears and aluminum parts with a fully functional table. He selected aluminum instead of steel because it was cheaper, and he could cut it himself. When not in use, the extra leaves can hang on the wall as sculpture. In order to get a better view of the legs, he set a piece of Plexiglas into the tabletop and allowed the legs to penetrate the surface. To give them function, the legs hold turned dining accessories, including a salad bowl, a cruet set, candelabra, salt and pepper shakers, and scientific glassware doubling as wine carafes and vases.

The table typifies the 1970s aesthetic that favored massive, dark surfaces with lots of curves and bold shapes. McCarthy made the piece for the 1977 Young Americans competition sponsored by the American Crafts Council, where it won an award. He gave up studio furniture twenty years ago and now does mostly architectural commissions in Sonoma, California.

JUDY KENSLEY MCKIE

born 1944
Boston, Massachusetts

Monkey Settee

1995, walnut and cast bronze, 35 ½ × 71 ¾ × 24. Gift of the James Renwick Alliance in honor of Michael W. Monroe, Renwick Gallery curator-in-charge, 1986–1995, 1995.67

ALTHOUGH TRAINED IN THE FINE ARTS AT THE RHODE Island School of Design, Judy McKie is known for the sculpted animal furniture she creates in her shop in Cambridge, Massachusetts. A self-trained woodworker, she started out making simple furniture for her own use and then began to decorate it to make it more personal—like decorated Pennsylvania German boxes that often had children's names on them. At the urging of her friend, Garry Knox Bennett, McKie began experimenting with bronze casting. "Metal gives a sense of permanence and age," she observed, and it allows her to produce limited editions.[39]

The cast bronze monkeys that form the arms and back of this bench are attached to a joined walnut base. She carved the monkeys in plaster from which the castings were made. She is influenced by African art as well as pre-Columbian, aboriginal, and ancient Egyptian and Greek art and artifacts. McKie's *Monkey Settee* is inspired by monkeys carved on West African throne chairs. McKie's animals have a certain edge. They are altered, so as to be a little mysterious. They look right at you, aloof and not quite naturalistic. The symmetrical pairs emphasize the duality of the animals' character, friendly maybe, but slightly menacing. Lately, McKie has collaborated with jeweler Tim McClelland to incorporate some of her animal imagery into jewelry.

[39] Goodison, *Sit Up and Take Notice!* Essay about Judy Kensley McKie.

DAVID MERRIFIELD

born 1968
Detroit, Michigan

*Tea Cabinet**

2002, steel, cherry, and walnut, 62 × 38 × 15. Gift of the James Renwick Alliance, Karen Johnson Boyd, Lois and Richard England, Colleen and John Kotelly, the Smithsonian Women's Committee, and the artist, 2002.45a–f

TRAINED AS AN ENGINEER, DAVID MERRIFIELD IS a self-taught cabinetmaker working in Fairview, North Carolina. He made this cabinet, which incorporates design elements drawing upon his engineering study, as a display case for a tea set. With the top rising up and the bottom falling away, the angles create a sense of tension and contrast with the three cantilevered, horizontal shelves holding the tea service on the inside. He bought the traditional Chinese clay tea set from an importer. The two other cabinets in the series have a rectangular case without the angles and are less successful. The arch over the stone on the interior suggests Japanese architecture. In addition to Japanese proportions and balance, Merrifield's work also exhibits the lightness of Shaker design and the angularity, though not the massiveness, of turn-of-the-century arts-and-crafts furniture.

Reflecting his engineering background, the sandblasted steel frame presents a light appearance and provides a dramatic contrast with the red cherry side panels and the brown walnut shelves. Supported on thin steel legs, the cabinet seems to float in space, accentuating its dramatic lines. The cabinet won Best in Show at the 2002 *Smithsonian Craft Show* and was selected by Kenneth Trapp to be acquired for the Renwick's permanent collection.

NORMA MINKOWITZ

born 1937
New York City

*The Landscape of My Mind**

1976–78, knitted, crocheted, and padded cotton and silk with wood, chair: 32 × 31 × 32; ottoman: 7 × 29 × 35. Gift of the artist, 1982.45a–b

A GRADUATE OF NEW YORK CITY'S COOPER UNION School of Art in the late 1950s, Norma Minkowitz initially focused on pen-and-ink portraits. During the 1970s, she resurrected the skill of crocheting she had learned as a child and began making clothing, soft sculptures, and wall hangings. She wanted to draw with fiber. At the time, Minkowitz was making mostly small fiber objects, but she kept looking at this chair and imagining it becoming a landscape. Using crochet, knitting, and padding, she created a fantasy landscape. The design evolved and was not preplanned or sketched.[40] The finials on the chair suggest mountains, and she carries out that theme with padded triangles on the back. The small gray circular shapes refer to shale; the large circles on the back depict caverns; and the cascading needlework down the back suggests a waterfall. The billowing skirt at the bottom conjures up the image of a river flowing out of a cave. She made the ottoman to fit into the chair to continue the line of the arms, but it also recalls a giant seashell or rock. "Norma" is stitched into the fabric on the floor below the arm. A renowned fiber artist, Minkowitz has made only one chair.

The piece represents an important milestone in Minkowitz's work as it evolved from small needlework to larger sculptural pieces. This early effort is opaque, while her lacelike open work since the 1980s is transparent. More recently, her pieces are usually crocheted around a form. The form is removed after the fiber is stiffened with shellac. Lloyd Herman, the first director of the Renwick Gallery, saw her chair and asked her to donate it to the museum. Having no place to put it in her house, she happily obliged. Kenneth Trapp added two of her crocheted vessels to the collection in 1990s. Minkowitz works in Westport, Connecticut.

[40] Norma Minkowitz, telephone interview with the author, August 17, 2005.

SHINICHI MIYAZAKI

born 1939
Tokyo, Japan

*Armchair**

1975, oak, teak, leather, and brass, 29 ½ × 24 × 26.
Museum purchase, 1975.173

SHINICHI MIYAZAKI TRAINED AS A PAINTER IN JAPAN and immigrated in 1967, working first as an assistant to sculptor Minoru Niizuma in New York City. Eventually, Miyazaki set up his own shop, where he designed and built furniture and created fine interior woodworking. At one point, he made full-scale models for sculptor Isamu Noguchi. In the late 1970s, he turned to making hand-dyed, down-filled coats with his first wife, a textile designer. In the early 1980s, he returned to woodworking full time, and in 1991, began specializing in elegant wood handbags inspired by traditional Japanese carrying bags. Since 2003, Miyazaki has again focused mainly on furniture and sculpture in his shop in rural Massachusetts.

He submitted *Armchair* to *Craft Multiples*, an exhibition organized in 1975 by the Renwick Gallery, which purchased it shortly thereafter. The leather upholstery passes through slots in the rails and is held with dowels inserted through sewn sleeves. The seat and crest rails are attached to the frame with through tenons fastened by teak keys. The oak side pieces are joined with unique curvilinear joints, a reference to traditionally complex Japanese joinery, which is both decorative and functional. Although the chair is easily reproducible, Miyazaki only made a few copies before moving on to other projects.

GEORGE NAKASHIMA

1905 Spokane, Washington
1990 New Hope, Pennsylvania

Lounge Chair

about 1969, walnut with hickory spindles and legs, 33 ⅛ × 23 ½ × 25. Transfer from the National Museum of American History, Smithsonian Institution, 2004.34

TRAINED AS AN ARCHITECT AT THE UNIVERSITY OF Washington and the Massachusetts Institute of Technology, George Nakashima learned cabinetmaking while held at a Japanese-American internment camp during World War II. Released in 1943, he settled in New Hope, Pennsylvania, and opened a cabinet shop. Beginning in the 1940s, Nakashima made all of his furniture himself, but gradually his studio expanded. He began to issue catalogues, which by the 1980s contained more than seventy-five designs. At its peak, his workshop employed about a dozen craftsmen.

In 1970, the Smithsonian's Museum of History and Technology (now the National Museum of American History) ordered a set of eight of the lounge chairs from Nakashima Studios to furnish a public seating area. After almost twenty-five years of use, this one was transformed from utilitarian furniture to museum artifact when it was transferred to the Renwick collection.

The design for the splayed legs and the seat derive from Nakashima's straight-back chair of the 1940s, while the crest rail resembles the one on his famous 1950 *Mira Chair,* named for his daughter (who took over the firm after her father's death). In the late 1950s, Nakashima designed the "Origins" collection for the Grand Rapids furniture company Widdicomb-Mueller. *Lounge Chair,* produced a decade later, closely resembled chairs in that series, but the stretchers could be eliminated on the lounge chair. Its legs were short and sturdy compared to the more fragile legs on his taller chairs.

GEORGE NAKASHIMA

*Conoid Chair**

1971, walnut and hickory, 35 ⅛ × 20 ⅝ × 18 ¾. Gift of Lloyd E. Herman, founding director and director emeritus of the Renwick Gallery (1971–1986), 1991.125

MUCH OF NAKASHIMA'S WORK WAS DESIGNED around massive slabs of wood he and the client would personally select from his vast storage sheds. Other pieces, like *Conoid Chair,* were stock items assembled from pre-cut parts after an order was taken. He developed the *Conoid Chair* in 1959, shortly after he had built his innovative studio with a conoid-shaped roof. The walnut legs were cut and shaped from a flat piece of wood, and the hickory spindles were roughed out on a lathe and then hand shaved in much the same way Windsor chairs were fabricated in the eighteenth century. The chair has only two legs, but it slides on runners that work well on carpeted floors, which were popular in the 1950s and 1960s. The cantilever concept pays homage to the first tubular steel, cantilevered side chairs designed by Marcel Breuer and Mart Stam in 1927. Although Nakashima made several thousand *Conoid Chairs* over the course of his career, each one differed because of the unique grain of the wood.

GEORGE NAKASHIMA

Conoid Bench

1977, walnut and hickory, 31 ⅛ × 84 ½ × 35 ⅝.
Gift of Dr. and Mrs. Warren D. Brill, 1991.121

LIKE NAKASHIMA'S *CONOID CHAIR*, THE NAME OF this bench derives from the conoid-shaped roof on his studio. Shaped hickory spindles form the backs of both the bench and the chair, but there the similarity ends. The seat of the bench is a large slab of walnut carefully selected for a specific client, George Flavin of Garrett Park, Maryland, whose name is inked on the bottom. Similar walnut slabs were incorporated into Nakashima's signature desk, table, and cabinet tops. He cut the tops in irregular shapes to take advantage of the prominent grain pattern and frequently left a strip of light sapwood to highlight the edges. In an era dominated by mass production, Nakashima sought to maintain a connection with the raw materials harvested from nature. To hold the weight of the walnut slab, the bench is supported on four turned walnut legs.

CRAIG NUTT

born 1950
Belmond, Iowa

Radish Salad Bowl

1998, maple, birch, and tupelo, 55 ⅝ × 21 × 21.
Gift of the James Renwick Alliance, 1999.5a–l

IS *RADISH SALAD BOWL* FURNITURE? IT QUALIFIES ON several counts. It is a container; it serves a culinary function, as does much specialized furniture; and it is based on the common eighteenth-century tripod table form. Indeed, Craig Nutt saw many tripod tables when he built antique reproductions and worked as a furniture restorer. He taught himself the skills after graduating from the University of Alabama with a religion degree in 1972.

For this "vege table," three cayenne peppers made of tupelo support a lathe-turned maple radish that separates into a pair of salad bowls.[41] The radish leaves, carved out of birch, become salad servers. The confection was inspired by an earlier, unpainted version made for a friend who liked Caesar salads, even though Caesar salads do not contain radishes. Because Nutt decorated and sealed the piece with nontoxic paints and nontoxic urethane, it can safely contain food. Nutt lacquered a few of his earlier pieces with pure colors, but soon made liberal use of shading to make the vegetables appear as realistic as possible.

Nutt's interest in vegetables may have started in college, where he joined a group of creative musicians who dressed up as vegetables and played homemade instruments. He is also an avid ornamental gardener. Upon hearing Vice President George H.W. Bush in the 1988 presidential campaign state he would not use food as a weapon, he began making vegetable bombs. After seeing whirligigs at the Kentuck Museum near his home in Northport, Alabama, he expanded his repertoire to include vegetable whirligigs; it was a short jump to vegetable furniture. He now lives in Kingston Springs, Tennessee, near Nashville.

Nutt's latest *Radish Table* 2004 rests on frilly leaves, suggesting ballroom dance gowns. Always drawing on historical furniture, he thought of a drop-leaf table and decided to "have the leaves drop up and gain access to the inside of my radish."[42]

---

[41] Craig Nutt, telephone interview with the author, January 2007. "Vege table" is Nutt's description.

[42] "Commissions," *American Craft* 65, no. 4 (August–September 2005): 25.

JERE OSGOOD

born 1936
New York City

Cylinder-Front Desk

1989, Australian lacewood, Honduran rosewood, pearwood, mahogany plywood, and Indonesian water buffalo calfskin, 45 ⅞ × 43 ¼ × 29. Gift of the James Renwick Alliance and museum purchase made possible by the Smithsonian Institution Collections Acquisition Program, 1990.53

JERE OSGOOD STARTED MAKING AND REPAIRING furniture in his father's basement shop as a teenager. He first attended the University of Illinois to become an architect but gave it up to pursue life as a furniture maker. He studied under Tage Frid at the School for American Craftsmen at the Rochester Institute of Technology and spent a year working in Denmark. Initially making only small items like boxes, trays, and modest tables, Osgood began to experiment with larger pieces in the late 1960s.

Inspired by tree roots, Osgood developed the technique of bent lamination, cutting boards into thin strips and then gluing them back together over forms to create shapes impossible to achieve in solid wood. He used the technique for the legs of *Cylinder-Front Desk*, which he made for the *New American Furniture* exhibition at the Museum of Fine Arts, Boston in 1989. He chose as his inspiration a Federal cylinder desk made in Salem, Massachusetts, between 1790 and 1800.[43] He fashioned the gently swelling side panels by bending and clamping multiple layers of thin wood over a curved form.

The interior—richer and more complex than most of his desks—features light pearwood above the drawers, rosewood for the drawers and dividers, and red-stained leather for the writing surface. Heeding his father's dictum, "If you need something, make it," Osgood even cut out the lid mechanism from flat brass plates.[44]

After holding faculty positions at the Philadelphia College of Art, Rochester Institute of Technology, and the Boston University Program in Artisanry, Osgood gave up teaching in 1985, when the latter program closed, to work full-time at his craft. Since then, he has primarily made variations of his signature elliptical desk at his studio in Wilton, New Hampshire.

[43] Cooke, *New American Furniture*, 88–91.

[44] Ibid., 88.

ALBERT PALEY

born 1944
Philadelphia, Pennsylvania

Lectern

1990, forged steel, brass, and copper, 47 × 34 × 22.
Gift of Peter T. Joseph, 1998.34.3

AFTER ALBERT PALEY GRADUATED FROM THE TYLER School of Art at Temple University, he started his career making jewelry. However, after winning the competition for the *Portal Gates* at the Renwick in 1974, he became famous for his forged-steel structures. After a period of creating furniture and decorative arts, he has, for the past twenty-five years, focused mostly on producing large-scale, site-specific sculpture at his studio in Rochester, New York.

Paley designed his first lectern in 1971 and has made a half-dozen variations since. This example with a brass and copper top, was one of a series of ten, each slightly different, Paley made in 1989 and 1990. One of Paley's favorite forms, a lectern from the series remains part of his personal collection. It is right at home with Paley's period art nouveau objects that he has collected since his teenage years and that serve as an obvious inspiration for much of his twisted and organically shaped work.

Once the main elements of the composition were prefabricated—the banner, the top, and the base—Paley shaped and welded the parts together, altering the composition as he went along. He likens the process to an impromptu conversation. Paley aims for an overall gestural effect of fluidity, balance, and counterpoint between the parts in the manner of an abstract expressionist painter. After he assembles the piece and grinds the welds smooth, the lectern is sandblasted and a patina is applied. The lectern, like his popular plant stands, has a blackened, chemical patina that requires waxing to prevent oxidation. Other pieces he coated with a metallic paint so the surface color would not change. The lecterns and plant stands required several weeks to fabricate, but he spread the process over a period of approximately six months.

STEPHEN PERRIN

born 1948
Detroit, Michigan

*Folding Wall Chairs**

1992, maple, bird's-eye maple, tiger maple, cherry, walnut, and aniline dyes, 43 × 17 × 4 each. Gift of MCI, 2001.89.4.1–4

AFTER WORKING FOR TWENTY YEARS AS A GRAPHIC designer in television, Stephen Perrin decided to extend his creative talents into making studio furniture in Baltimore, Maryland. He studied cabinetmaking with Michael Pierschalla, a graduate of the Rochester Institute of Technology. Perrin then refined his technique at the Haystack Mountain School of Crafts in Deer Isle, Maine, and launched his career with a show at the Meredith Gallery in Baltimore. The influence of Pierschalla is evident in *Folding Wall Chairs*, which take on a cubist or deconstructionist appearance.

Perrin's first versions of the chairs were non-functional wall sculptures. The idea of hanging furniture on the wall dates back at least to the nineteenth century, when the Shakers routinely hung their ladder-back chairs and other items on rows of pegs lining their walls. Tom Loeser, in 1988, made a similar series of wall-hung chairs, but his had a geometric, high-tech design.

Two of Perrin's *Folding Wall Chairs* refer to early eighteenth-century William-and-Mary style ladder-back chairs, and the other two relate to typical, vernacular ones made throughout the eighteenth and nineteenth centuries, and even today. Each of his chairs was produced in a different wood and then stained with red and green aniline dyes that, on these examples, have faded in the sun. They once hung on a wall near a window in the MCI corporate café before being donated to the Renwick.

TIMOTHY PHILBRICK

born 1952
Providence, Rhode Island

*Curly Cherry Cellaret**

1994, cherry, satinwood, and fossil ivory, 54 × 41½ × 22.
Gift of Dr. and Mrs. Joseph A. Chazan, 1997.43

TIMOTHY PHILBRICK RECEIVED A SOLID GROUNDING in historical furniture styles, first as an apprentice to John C. Northup Jr., an antique restorer and reproduction specialist in Rhode Island, and then from furniture historian John Kirk in the Program in Artisanry at Boston University. Philbrick now works in Narragansett, Rhode Island. In *Curly Cherry Cellaret,* he used a whole-number proportioning system that was loosely inspired by a cellaret illustrated in Thomas Sheraton's late eighteenth-century *The Cabinet-Maker and Upholsterer's Drawing-Book.* A careful student of traditional proportions, Philbrick published a seminal article in *Fine Woodworking* on classical systems used to design eighteenth-century American furniture.[45]

The legs, hand-shaped from solid pieces of wood, are attached to the corners of the case in the manner of Émile-Jacques Ruhlmann's art deco furniture from the 1920s. This tambour, his first and only one, hides a fold-down writing surface big enough for storing wine bottles or liquor in the back. Because the work surface would be exposed for long periods, he believed the tambour was more attractive than a pair of doors. His work typifies the growing importance that historical revivals play in recent studio furniture design.

[45] Timothy Philbrick, "Tall Chests: The Art of Proportioning," *Fine Woodworking,* no. 9 (Winter 1977): 39–43.

PETER PIEROBON

born 1957
Vancouver, Canada

Time Totem

1993, ebonized mahogany, 95 × 25 × 20.
Gift of MCI, 2001.89.2

TIME TOTEM, WHICH STANDS NEARLY EIGHT FEET tall, was designed specifically for the lobby of the MCI corporate headquarters in Washington, D.C. Working with the Renwick's Curator-in-Charge Michael Monroe, who was advising MCI at the time, Pierobon completed the three-piece commission in about seven weeks of twelve-hour days. Two clocks were intended to stand near the elevators, while the one in the Renwick collection, a foot taller, stood in the atrium.

For the two smaller clocks, Pierobon carved zigzag shapes in ebonized mahogany that flanked a fish-shaped central section. The technique evoked the black argillite carvings of the Haida Indians from Pierobon's birthplace in Vancouver, British Columbia, near his current home. The Renwick clock, lacking the zigzag sections, features Pierobon's signature glyphs, based on Gregg shorthand, carved on the front. The musings on the passage of time are translated and inscribed on the back. As Pierobon observed, "The surface of my work is overrun with tool marks and symbols."[46] He liked the way light played off the black surfaces in contrast to the effects of light on the naturally finished and intricately carved central section. The M&M-shaped dials recall similar faces on some of Castle's tall clocks.

Pierobon trained at the Wendell Castle School in upstate New York and worked for Castle after graduation in the mid-1980s, during which time Castle was completing his famous clock series. Pierobon thought the clock motif was especially appropriate for a company that had branches worldwide in many different time zones.

---

[46] Hosaluk, *Scratching the Surface*, 49.

PETER PITTMAN

born 1953
Prentiss, Mississippi

b-ReIk.iNtHE~'sIstaM...D-vii/O.13

2000, painted wood, metal, and fabric, 58 ¼ × 24 ½ × 23. Gift of Alexander P. Fritzinger-Pittman, Nicholas A. Fritzinger-Pittman, and Connell Gallery, 2001.29

THE MATHEMATICAL RELATIONSHIPS AND THE architectonic quality of this carefully constructed composition reflect Peter Pittman's profession as a practicing architect in Atlanta, Georgia. He trained at the École des Beaux Arts in Paris and at Georgia Tech. This piece was the last of seven in a series of chairs. He starts with found chairs because they are very personal objects, and everyone can easily relate to them. While he likes people to bring their own interpretation to his work, the title *Break in the System* (rendered in the phonetic spelling) suggests a starting point. The design was inspired by his two sons' learning to read. Breaks between letters form words, and words form sentences and paragraphs to convey ideas. Similarly, all the parts of the chair, front and back, convey a concept that can then be interpreted.[47]

The chair is packed with information—much like the contemporary environment, which is overloaded with data. For example, the ceramic angel, God's messenger, announces that the chair carries important messages. The chair itself is a metaphor for a throne from which royal pronouncements might emanate, suggesting a possible source for the cryptic messages it embodies. The unpainted block on the seat echoes in miniature the throne idea. One prominent theme is that of a container. The chair is a container for the body. The urn is another container, perhaps for ashes of the body. The gray paint covering the chair unifies the composition and calms the feelings generated by information overload. On another level, the color evokes the idea of a mysterious scrim that obscures meaning, similar to Pittman's obscuring his own intentions, so the viewer must work to understand his compositions.

Pittman's assemblages bring to mind the analogous work of Louise Nevelson from the late 1950s and 1960s, which in turn owes a debt to the earlier Dadaists and surrealists. Both Pittman and Nevelson collected the detritus of the past to evoke specific themes. While Nevelson encased the objects in boxes as abstract sculpture, Pittman attaches them to the icon of a chair, which gives them a different structure and symbolic meaning. A closer look at the work of both artists reveals their attempts to create order out of seeming chaos. Although the elements encrusting Pittman's chair are ritualistic and symbolic, they also create order with their multiple harmonic forms and textures.

[47] Peter Pittman, interview with the author, July 27, 2005.

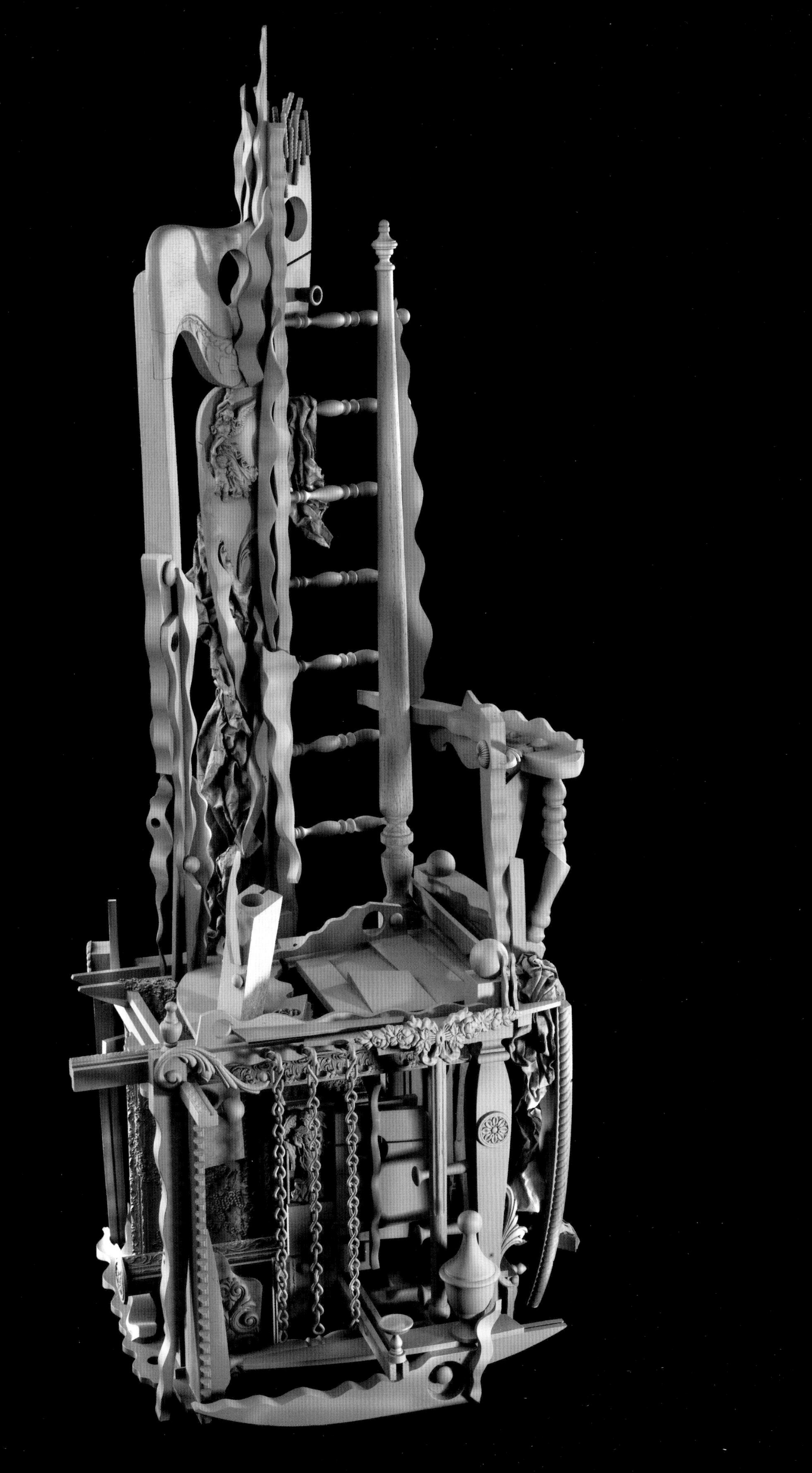

CHARLES RADTKE

born 1964
Hermann, Missouri

*Sarcophagus Cabinet #1**

1999, mahogany, sassafras, and brass, 44 × 18 × 30.
Gift of John and Robyn Horn, 2000.14

CHARLES RADTKE LEARNED CABINETMAKING AT THE St. Paschal Friary in Illinois while working on a degree in computer science and now resides in Cedarburg, Wisconsin. He studied one summer with James Krenov at Anderson Ranch Arts Center in Colorado, where he learned the virtues of exacting workmanship and a love of cabinets on legs. Rather than using the carved wooden pulls favored by Krenov, Radtke fabricated textured brass hardware for *Sarcophagus Cabinet #1*. Others who influenced his work include Charles Rennie Mackintosh, Émile-Jacques Ruhlmann, and Louis Sullivan. From Mackintosh, he learned an appreciation for subtle details; from Ruhlmann, a love of opulent materials; and from Sullivan, a preference for pattern and repetition.

The idea for the "Sarcophagus Cabinet" series came after seeing an ancient Egyptian sarcophagus at the Metropolitan Museum of Art in New York City. Radtke was impressed with the blocks at the bottom of the stone case and incorporated that idea into the wooden brackets just under the top.[48] The detail also alludes to similar brackets found in the buildings designed by Charles and Henry Greene in California before World War I. As in most of his work, Radtke laid out the spacing for the brackets solely by eye. Yet the spacing bears an uncanny relationship to the Fibonacci progression, wherein each number in a series is the sum of the previous two numbers.

Like George Nakashima, Radtke selects only the most highly figured wood for his work. He already had the Cuban mahogany on hand, and the sassafras came from a farm near his boyhood home in Missouri. The horizontal and vertical book-matching of the sassafras creates a dramatic sense of tension and mystery.[49] Ten to twenty coats of tung oil, applied over a scraped, vice-sanded surface, bring out the best in the grain of the wood.

[48] Charles Radtke, written response to interview questions, received April 26, 2004.

[49] Book-matching involves cutting two sheets of veneer from the same board so that the grain pattern in one sheet is the mirror image of the other.

JIM ROSE

born 1966
Beach Grove, Indiana

*No. 56 Seven-Drawer Counter**

1997, steel with natural rust patina, 33 ⅝ × 60 ⅜ × 27 ⅜.
Gift of the artist and his wife, 2000.40

JIM ROSE RECEIVED HIS BFA IN SCULPTURE FROM THE School of the Art Institute of Chicago in 1988. Soon thereafter, he started making art furniture on a trial-and-error basis, because he had not taken a furniture design class.[50] Following visits to several Shaker communities in New England in the 1990s, he started to make interpretations of Shaker furniture in steel. This is the fifty-sixth piece in that series, which now numbers more than 250.

Slightly larger than the original, this example is based on a cabinet attributed to Grove Wright working at the Hancock Shaker community in Massachusetts in the 1830s. Using eighth-inch steel, Rose welded a rim around the top edge to suggest the thicker wood used in the original. It can take him up to three months to find the right piece of steel because he uses the same care a cabinetmaker takes in selecting the right piece of wood. The natural patina on the metal recalls the original Shaker finish. Rose's most recent work includes pieces inspired by Chinese design and by contemporary African American quilts of Gee's Bend, Alabama. He works in Forestville, Wisconsin.

[50] Jim Rose, telephone interview with Betsy Davison, December 20, 2004.

CHRISTOPHER SABIN

born 1941
Brockton, Massachusetts

Three-Legged Stool

1974, white ash and maple, 28 ¾ × 14 ⅛ × 14 ⅛. Museum purchase, 1975.176

THREE-LEGGED STOOL BY CHRISTOPHER SABIN OF Greenfield, New Hampshire, has a hard-edged and controlled appearance. The ash legs are mortised and tenoned into the shaped maple seat. Steam-bent stretchers strengthen the long legs. He made it for the *Craft Multiples* exhibition at the Renwick in 1975, and it was later purchased for the collection.

After receiving a Bachelor of Fine Arts degree in painting, Sabin apprenticed for two years to Hyacinth Renaud, a Vermont woodworker. Sabin's work shows the influence of the Shakers, Alvar Aalto, and Wharton Esherick, with a dash of Chinese design.

KIM SCHMAHMANN

born 1955
Johannesburg, South Africa

*Bureau of Bureaucracy**

1993–99, various hardwoods, veneers, mother-of-pearl, gold leaf, and brass, 96 × 36 × 24. Gift of an anonymous donor, 2000.48a–h

BORN IN SOUTH AFRICA, KIM SCHMAHMANN trained as an architect before he came to Boston and attended the North Bennet Street School. He now resides in Cambridge, Massachusetts. *Bureau of Bureaucracy,* a tour de force of cabinet-making, is based on sixteenth-century northern European cabinets of curiosities. It is made up of seventeen different woods, has no straight lines, and took more than five years to complete.

This cabinet's design is a commentary on modern bureaucracies—often imposing and straightforward on the outside, but cunning, complex, and ambiguous on the inside. The twenty flat drawers in the bottom section contain important documents bureaucracies have created for Schmahmann, including his birth certificate, Social Security card, marriage license, diplomas, and even his blank death certificate.

The upper section recreates a niche in the reading room of the Library of Congress, an area that symbolizes a positive result of bureaucracy because it preserves the knowledge of mankind. Next to it, a shelf of four books conceals drawers—drawers with glass ceilings, drawers within drawers, false drawers, iron cage drawers, bottomless drawers, useless drawers, and even a back door—all representing the dark side of bureaucracies. Three hidden drawers contain codes, coins, money, jewelry, and a time capsule. On the bookshelf, a tattered *Humanity* is being squeezed by *Power,* and *Rationality* is turned upside down as a result of our modern society. The unnamed fourth volume represents, according to Schmahmann, "the unacknowledged conditions of our lives" that we take for granted but often do not appreciate.[51]

On the pull-out writing surface, Schmahmann has inlaid the Indian game of Snakes and Ladders. He modified the board by intertwining the snakes and ladders to make the point that vices and virtues are not always clear-cut. The numbered squares are not random, but arranged in a magic square—which was first designed by the Chinese—wherein numerals in each line, column, or diagonal add up to the same number.

The back of the cabinet is divided into three parts representing three different views of the world. The top depicts single-point perspective (focusing on the door that serves as the back door to bureaucracy). Schmahmann sees the Renaissance invention as the symbolic apogee of Western civilization. The center section shows a classical, fluted column rising from the rough tree trunk. Schmahmann says the image represents the duality of civilization: subject and object, body and soul, material and spiritual. The lowest section, made up of a series of patterned panels, represents Eastern civilizations and their multiple but interrelated perspectives. Placed at the bottom, it symbolizes the foundation of civilization, but also the disregard Westerners have typically shown for the East.

[51] Kim Schmahmann, undated brochure about *Bureau of Bureaucracy,* Schmahmann's artist file at the Renwick Gallery.

HUMANITY
RATIONALITY
WJD
1980

JOANNE SHIMA

born 1960
Long Island, New York

*Child's Chair**

1987, lacquered birch, maple, and medium density fiberboard, 13 × 12 × 21. Gift of Kenneth R. Trapp, 2000.55

JOANNE SHIMA WORKED AS AN ANTIQUE RESTORER and carpenter while taking fine woodworking classes at Bucks County Community College in Pennsylvania with Mark Sfirri, the well-known woodturner. After she completed that two-year program, Sfirri hired her as his shop assistant. Shima made *Child's Chair* while working for Sfirri, who joined the college in 1982, the year it began to offer a two-year associate's degree in fine woodworking. In her children's chairs, Shima recreates Oreo cookies and Tinker Toys at the corners of the chair seat, capturing the essence of childhood. Her daughter completed the decoration with a slightly different drawing on the back of each chair. Shima claimed the Renwick's example is her favorite. None of her subsequent furniture enjoyed the success of these pieces, and she has since left the studio furniture field.

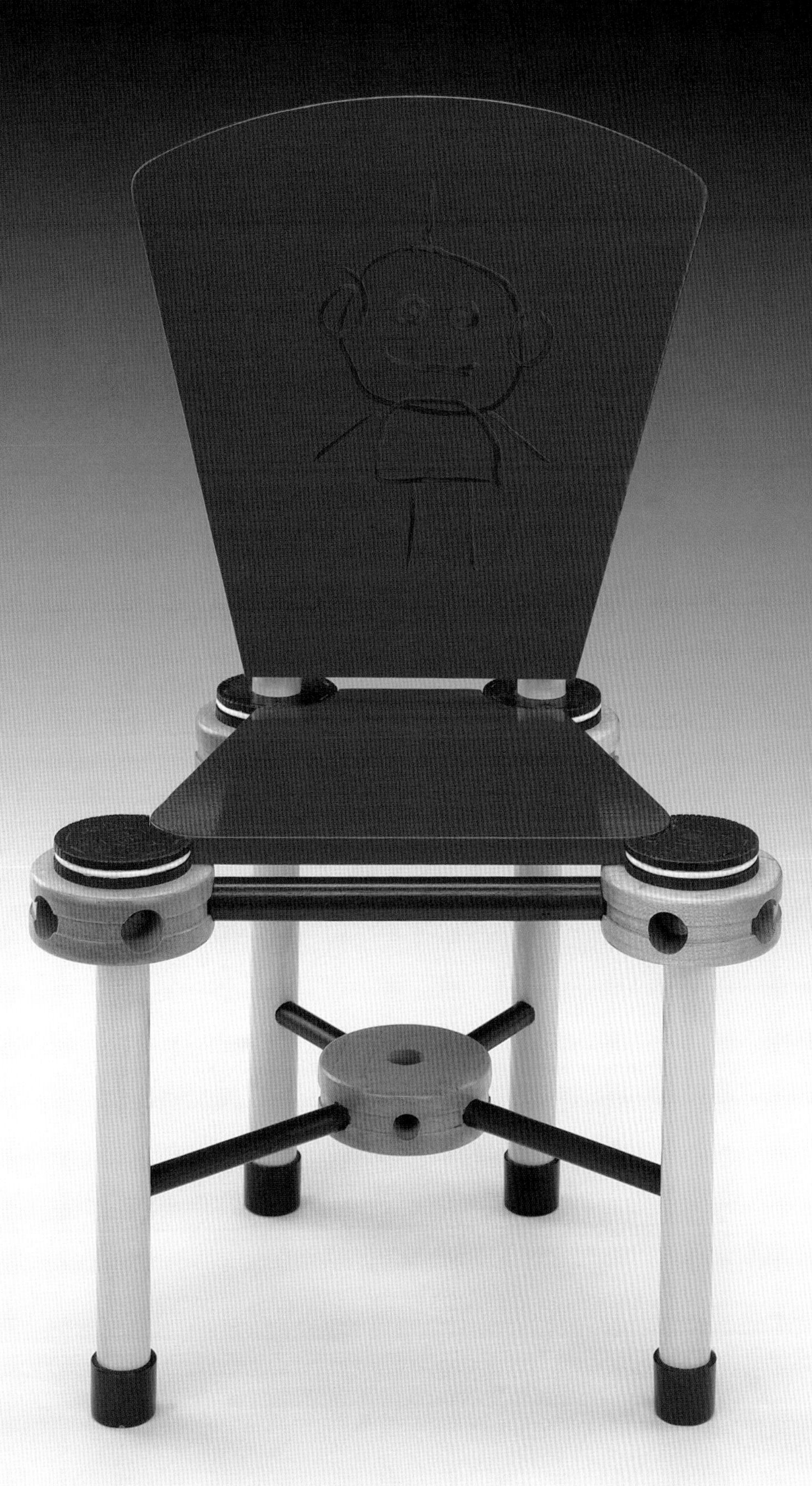

RANDY SHULL

born 1962
Sandwich, Illinois

*Ten**

1997, painted mahogany plywood, 18 × 58 × 31.
Gift of Diane and Marc Grainer, 2001.42

RANDY SHULL LEARNED THE BASICS OF WOODWORKING from his father and began selling his own furniture to classmates at the age of fifteen. He broadened his repertoire as a student at the Rochester Institute of Technology before settling in Asheville, North Carolina. Carved symbols, which have become a signature of his work, evolved from an interest in folk art. *Ten* refers to the ten symbolic shapes carved on the skirt of this coffee table. Some shapes are generic and take on whatever meaning the viewer chooses—such as the triangle, the inverted *V*, the *X*, and the concave ball. Others are specific, like the green house, a reference to his carpenter days with his father. The crescent recalls his trip to Turkey, where the symbol appears on the national flag. The fleur-de-lis symbolizes the city of Louisville, Kentucky, where his girlfriend lived. Shull assigned personal meanings to the blue tooth and heart—his symbols for spring and summer.

Shull developed a preference for a bright color palette after serving as an artist-in-residence at the artist colony at Altos de Chavon in the Dominican Republic.[52] He applies up to fifty coats of acrylic paint, carefully sanding between each to give the surface an aged look, but also to cover up the edges of the laminated plywood. The checkerboard pattern on the top vaguely refers to a game board. The elliptical top of *Ten* implies a subtle vaginal reference, one he repeats in other compositions.

[52] Randy Shull, telephone interview with Allison Byrd, November 2006.

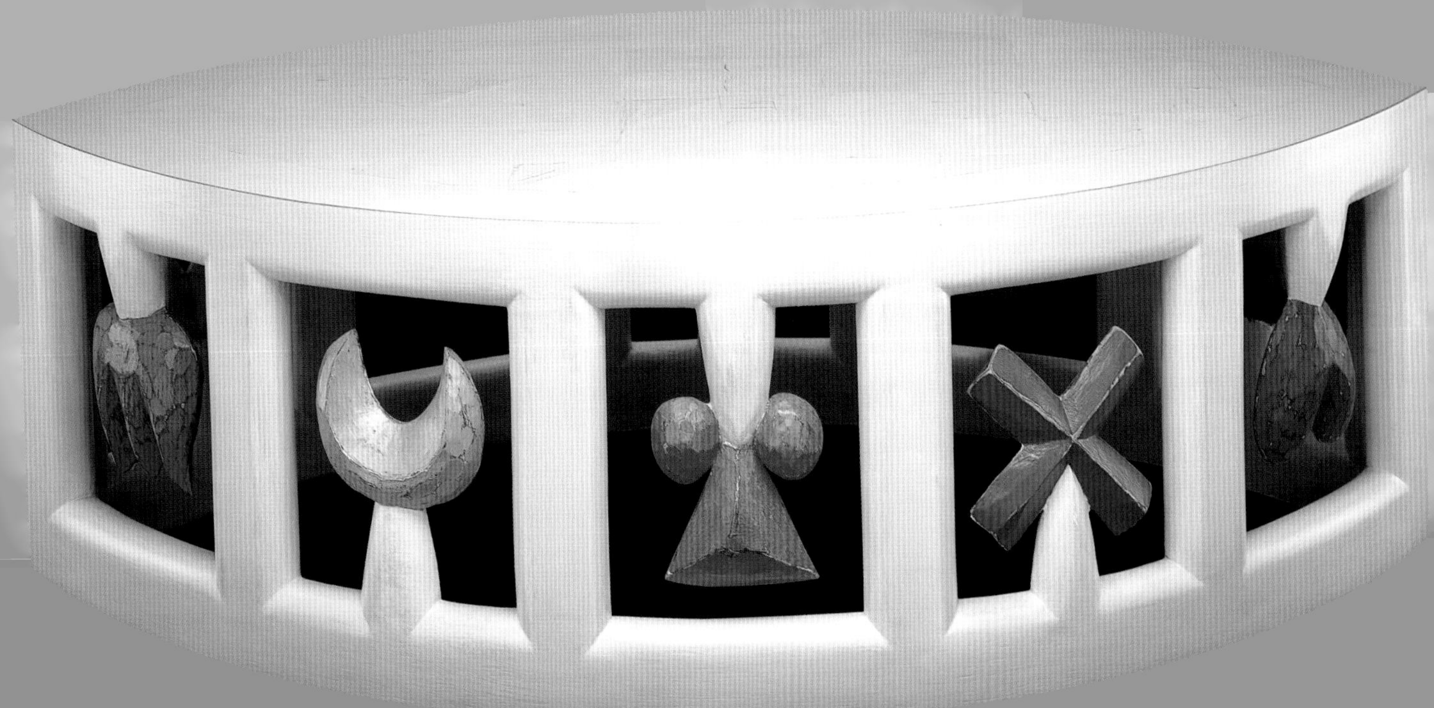

TOMMY SIMPSON

born 1939
Elgin, Illinois

Kiss the Cook

1992–1993, spalted maple, English oak, figured soft maple, lacewood, cherry, walnut, mahogany, and bone, 67 × 28 × 21. Gift of Daphne Farago, 2000.94

AFTER EARNING HIS MASTER'S DEGREE IN PAINTING in 1964 at the Cranbrook Academy of Art in Michigan, Tommy Simpson eventually settled in Washington, Connecticut. He has ventured into sculpture, jewelry, and ceramics as well as cabinetmaking. Daphne Farago commissioned *Kiss the Cook* for the kitchen in her house in Key West, Florida. "Don't Forget / To Kiss the Cook. / It's / An Old Family Recipe," a Farago family saying, is etched into the façade. The cabinet rests on legs carved in the shape of fish.

Reflecting his training as an artist, Simpson usually decorates his pieces with paint and carving. In *Kiss the Cook*, however, he inlaid the façade with a random pattern of at least seven different light and dark woods and then inset a tiny bone heart into the door. "People like the different wood samples, and it is a great way to use up scraps," he said.[53] Although it looks like a shallow cabinet, the back actually tapers to fit into a corner, so the drawers are shaped as trapezoids to maximize storage space.

As with most of his furniture, Simpson created a consciously unrefined quality in *Kiss the Cook*. The artist explained, "To achieve the spontaneous, approachable, childlike quality I enjoy, I liken my objects to the human body with all its flaws. For me, a focus on engineering stiffens my heart and limits my purpose."[54] Although Sam Maloof stands at the other end of the spectrum in terms of highly refined craftsmanship, Maloof was quoted as saying, "If I were to select a piece of contemporary furniture, it would be one of Tommy Simpson's."[55]

[53] Tommy Simpson, telephone interview with the author, September 2005.

[54] Tommy Simpson, telephone interview with the author, February 2, 2006, and email of that date. See also Cooke, *New American Furniture*, 114.

[55] Cooke, Ward, and L'Ecuyer, *The Maker's Hand*, 137.

DON'T FORGET
TO KISS THE COOK
IT'S
AN OLD FAMILY RECIPE

TOMMY SIMPSON

*G. W. Cabinet**

1994, poplar, basswood, metal, and gold foil with oil-based glaze, 74 × 33 × 19. Gift of the James Renwick Alliance, 1995.13

SIMILAR TO THE HIGHLY PERSONAL ASSEMBLAGES OF Joseph Cornell, Simpson's work is often strongly autobiographical. Simpson also borrows images from popular American culture, much like sculptor H. C. Westermann. The two ideas come together in *G. W. Cabinet,* which recalls a childhood skit in which Simpson played George Washington with not altogether positive memories.[56]

With several Simpson pieces to choose from, what could be more appropriate for the Renwick Gallery's national collection than one with a reference to George Washington? The cabinet takes the shape of the cherry tree from the Parson Weems myth. The work also suggests the form of a traditional papier-mâché candy dispenser Pennsylvania Germans gave to their children on holidays. The metal clasp is a logger's dog, used to hold logs together as they floated downriver to a sawmill. By carefully controlling the moisture content of the individual staves, Simpson hoped to ensure the coopered case would survive without cracking the painted surface.[57] As in most of his work, Simpson's aim in *G. W. Cabinet* is to share the joys—and sometimes the tribulations—of his life with others.

[56] Tommy Simpson, *Two Looks to Home: The Art of Tommy Simpson* (New York: Little, Brown & Company, 1999), 44.

[57] The case was made with narrow strips of wood with their edges cut on an angle so that when fitted together they form a cylinder in the same manner as barrel making (coopering). In coopering, it is important to insure that the pieces of wood all have the same moisture content, so that they expand and contract together.

EVERT SODERGREN

born 1920
Seattle, Washington

Sculptured Chair

designed 1953, built about 1975, walnut and leather, 30 × 28 × 24. Gift of Northwest Designer Craftsmen made possible by Deloris Tarzan Ament, Ralph and Shirley Anderson, Edith Fairhall, Diane and Marc Grainer, Anne Gould Houberg, Lloyd E. Herman, founding director and director emeritus of the Renwick Gallery (1971–1986), Alida and Christopher Lathan, Ramona Solberg, and the artist, 2004.12

EVERT SODERGREN BEGAN WORKING IN HIS FATHER'S cabinet shop making reproduction furniture at the age of fifteen, becoming the fourth generation of Sodergrens to enter the cabinetmaking trade. When his father returned to Sweden, he took over the shop.

Starting with the popular commercial Danish modern furniture of Finn Juhl and Hans Wegner of the 1950s, Sodergren wanted to design a chair that could not readily be mass produced. Experimenting for more than a year, he went through eight, full-scale prototypes before he was satisfied with the final product. The Renwick's *Sculptured Chair* derives from that prototype. The chair design, along with the *tansu* chest, developed in the 1970s, have become his signature pieces.

Few manufacturers would be willing to lavish the two hundred hours necessary to produce one of the chairs. First, Sodergren cut two giant splines out of aircraft-grade birch plywood in the shape of the two sides. The idea for the splines came from his early employment in the Boeing Airplane Company model shop, where he fabricated models using the technique.[58] He then cut the walnut and ebony parts for the arms and legs with a band saw. Sodergren used a router and shooting board to sculpt the general form and then sandwiched the parts onto the splines. The bent, laminated back support was attached to the back rail with a handmade brass hinge that allowed the back to adjust to the sitter. Hard ebony feet eliminated the need for protective metal glides. The chair was finished with a commercial impregnation finish—half oil and half naptha—that soaked into the wood. The original seat was webbed with leather and fitted with a one-inch foam cushion covered in leather. His more recent chairs substitute rubber for the leather webbing to increase resilience and comfort.

Since completing his first of these chairs in 1954, Sodergren has made more than two hundred of them, primarily in American black walnut, but also in woods ranging from teak and Honduran mahogany to oak (his least favorite). As with the metal fittings of his *tansu* chests, he makes all of the hardware himself. Unlike fellow first-generation cabinetmaker Sam Maloof, who takes pride in evolving his chairs over time, Sodergren strives for consistency. He once made a special oversized chair for a friend who was over six-feet tall and a set of undersized chairs for a houseboat, but they were exceptions. Now in his eighties, Sodergren recently retooled his shop in Seattle, Washington, with jigs and patterns to ensure a more uniform product as he turns more and more work over to apprentices.

[58] Evert Sodergren, interview with the author, July 27, 2005.

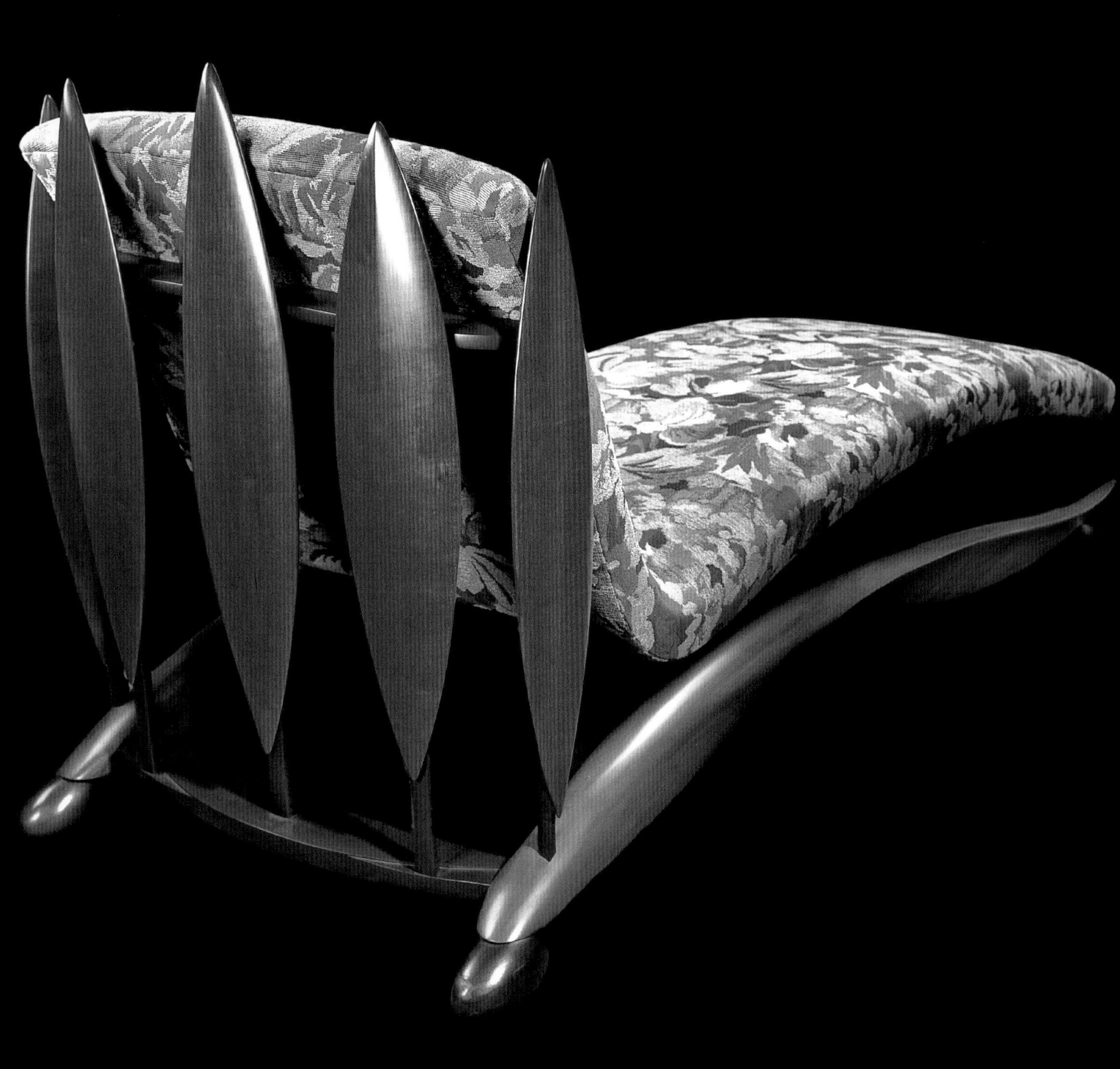

ROSANNE SOMERSON

born 1954
Philadelphia, Pennsylvania

*Botanical Reading Couch**

1992, painted mahogany and cherry with cotton, 39 × 75 ⅝ × 32 ¾.
Gift of the James Renwick Alliance, 1995.77

WHEN TAGE FRID TAUGHT ROSANNE SOMERSON at the Rhode Island School of Design, he once commented she had "ten thumbs." She nevertheless developed a strong technical background under his tutelage.[59] What distinguishes her furniture is it incorporates multiple levels of meaning. Somerson's goal is to draw viewers in with a pleasing composition and then hold their interest "by layering the work with levels of detail."[60]

After the birth of her daughter in 1988, Somerson took an interest in memories and nature, ideas she expressed in a series of benches and daybeds. *Botanical Reading Couch* recalls her childhood memory of reading under a willow tree. The hand-woven tapestry, made in Switzerland, suggests a pile of leaves, and the elliptical shapes on the back convey an even more explicit leaf reference. The horizontal supports for the couch evoke twisted tulip leaves, and the ovoid shapes they rest on seem to be rocks.[61] The hard wooden frame cradles the soft upholstered seat. The initials "M. W." on the frame belong to Mark Wessinger, who worked on the piece with her.

Through her furniture, Somerson reveals herself. She takes this same approach in her teaching. Somerson is head of the furniture design program at the Rhode Island School of Design, where she succeeded her mentor Tage Frid in 1985. She tries to get her students to identify their personal voices and to define themselves. And then she gives them the technical tools to express their ideas.

[59] Goodison, *Sit Up and Take Notice!* Essay about Rosanne Somerson.

[60] Edward S. Cooke Jr., "The Rise of Women Furniture Makers," *Woodwork* (April 2001): 71.

[61] Rosanne Somerson, telephone interview with the author, April 28, 2004.

ROSANNE SOMERSON

*When She Was Bad...**

1995, maple with rift white oak, pau amarello, glass, and handmade paper, 23 ¾ × 21 × 6 ¾. Gift of the James Renwick Alliance, 1995.32

FOLLOWING A STINT AS A WRITER AND EDITOR FOR *Fine Woodworking* magazine, Somerson began making furniture professionally in the late 1970s. After demonstrating her mastery of large furniture, she turned her creative energies to smaller pieces in the mid-1980s. Part of a series of jewelry cabinets she started making at that time, *When She Was Bad . . .* refers to the childhood rhyme "There was a little girl, / Who had a little curl, / Right in the middle of her forehead. / And when she was good, / She was very, very good. / But when she was bad, / She was horrid." The rhyme and the mirror play on notions of vanity. Somerson used a similar curl on a mirror she attached to a dressing table, a piece she exhibited in the 1993 *Earthly Delights* show at the Peter Joseph Gallery in New York City.

Somerson's work is typically full of surprises and can be interpreted on many different levels. She wants her furniture to trigger "a discovery process, possibly though visual connections, alignments, misalignments, or combinations of materials, sometimes with surprises in function or secrets."[62] Although she imbues her furniture with her own associations, she wants her work to evoke a personal meaning from the viewer as well.

In the Renwick's piece, Somerson sandblasted the glass outside the frame and silvered and stippled the maple frame with varied tones of white. She used plantation-grown yellowish pau amarello wood from Brazil for the drawer fronts and the darker oak for the cabinet. Her ingenious design features not only aesthetic rhythm, but also useful components. The curve of the top shelf echoes the curves of the drawers as well as those of the cabinet top. Yet it also serves the practical purpose of keeping earrings from falling off. In a final surprise, Somerson lined the bottoms and even the undersides of the drawers with handmade emerald green paper.

[62] Cooke, *New American Furniture*, 116.

JAY STANGER

born 1956
Boston, Massachusetts

*Bright City**

1987, painted curly maple and aluminum with pigskin, 49 × 21 × 19. Gift of Eleanor T. and Samuel J. Rosenfeld, 2002.8.14

BORN INTO A FAMILY OF ARTISTS, JAY STANGER trained at the Rochester Institute of Technology, the Leeds Design Workshop in Easthampton, Massachusetts, and the Program in Artisanry at Boston University. Although his work has been compared to cubist paintings or deconstructionist pieces, he claims he intends no art historical reference.[63]

Stanger resides outside of Boston in South Easton but goes into the city frequently. In this chair, he tries to capture the shapes of an urban environment. As is true in most of his work, Stanger in *Bright City* experimented with geometry and with different materials, including aluminum, maple, pigskin, and paint. Part of a series of chairs with similar shapes, this one is brightly painted, in contrast with others that feature unpainted exotic woods. Stanger fabricates all of the metal parts himself, except the bending and the anodizing of the aluminum.

[63] Jay Stanger, telephone interview with the author, August 2004.

MICHAEL STERLING

born 1948
Yuma, Arizona

*Chair**

1995, claro walnut, macassar ebony, putumuju, and leather, 54 ⅜ × 21 ¼ × 19 ⅜.
Gift of the artist in honor of Vanessa, Janna, and Tyler, 1998.73

MICHAEL STERLING TAUGHT HIMSELF WOODWORKING, largely from books, such as Ernest Joyce's *Encyclopedia of Furniture Making* and writings by James Krenov, who Sterling says, "captured for this upcoming generation the passion and soul of woodworking."[64] On occasion, he also attended workshops by Wendell Castle, Garry Knox Bennett, Tage Frid, and others. Most of Sterling's furniture is heavily influenced by the arts-and-crafts movement of the early twentieth century, especially the work of nineteenth-century English designer Edward Barnsley.

In *Chair*, Sterling began with a Frank Lloyd Wright chair design, but he slanted the slats in the back for comfort, something Wright rarely considered. An article in *Fine Woodworking* magazine on how to make a Chippendale chair provided useful technical information on dimensions, proportions, tenon size, angles, and other construction details. Inspired by Krenov's admonition to cut your own wood, Sterling harvested a claro walnut tree that grows only in the unique climate around Chico, California, about a hundred miles north of his Sacramento home. The piece of walnut he selected for the crest rail features an interesting basket weave pattern. The red and yellow flecks in the slats made from South American putumuju wood contrast with the orange, black, and gray in the walnut used for the rest of the chair. Sterling always includes some ebony in his work, and here he used it for the half-round molding outlining the seat rail. He made *Chair* as an extra while completing a commission for a dining room table and a set of matching chairs.[65] He divides his time between a career as an emergency-room nurse and a cabinetmaker, creating a half-dozen commissions and speculative pieces a year.

[64] Michael Sterling, email to author, February 2, 2006.

[65] Michael Sterling, telephone interview with the author, April 2004.

MARA SUPERIOR

born 1951
New York City

ROY SUPERIOR

born 1934
New York City

*Aqua Vitae**

1986 (porcelain) and 1990 (cabinet), painted birch plywood with 23k gold leaf, bone, glass, and metal with handmade porcelain vase, overall: 78 5/8 × 38 1/4 × 14 1/4; porcelain sculpture: 13 5/8 × 14 3/4 × 4 1/2; porcelain base: 2 1/8 × 14 3/4 × 6 3/8. Gift of the James Renwick Alliance, 1996.39a–c

AQUA VITAE, ONE OF A SERIES OF COLLABORATIONS between ceramic artist Mara Superior and her husband, Roy, celebrates sea life. Others in the series also pay homage to nature, such as *Arbor Vitae* (trees), *La Mer* (ocean), and *Botanica* (plants). Sometimes the themes are conceived before the porcelains are fired or, as in the case of *Aqua Vitae*, the cabinet was built to complement the finished ceramics. Given the unpredictable nature of a porcelain vase in the kiln, Roy observes it is unwise to build the house for the vase until the porcelain is fired. The decorations on the porcelain refer to nineteenth-century European trade with the Far East and include Chinese ginger jars, Canton china, and shipping crates. The title of Mara's vessel, *Alla Porcella*, or "like a shiny seashell," derives from Marco Polo's first description of the qualities of porcelain.

Roy decorated the cabinet surface using traditional grain-painting techniques, employing dry pigments dissolved in vinegar or stale beer applied over a solid ground color. He then textured the paint with combs, brushes, and his fingers and sealed it with a clear finish. The cabinet door serves as the frame for his oil painting of a salmon, and above the vase, he carved and painted fish (cod, hake, and pollock), not unlike antique ice-fishing decoys. He continued the fish motif with the carved and scrimshawed bone knob and latch and fish-shaped brass hinges. The zigzag pattern on the crest of the cabinet and around the upper section comes from the Egyptian hieroglyph for water.

Roy, with a master's degree from Yale University in painting and printmaking, is self taught in woodworking. He has headed the wood program at the University of the Arts in Philadelphia since 1990. Mostly known for his miniature-scaled sculptural objects, Roy's work usually incorporates paintings, as well as wood and metal.

AQUA VITAE

JON SUTTER

born 1965
Ithaca, New York

*Under Continuous Monitor**

2000, painted birch and poplar plywood and poplar with concrete, aluminum, and found objects, 33 × 10 ½ × 7. Gift of David Michaelis and Clara Bingham in honor of Michael Michaelis, 2001.22

DRAWING ON HIS EXPERIENCE AS A MAKER OF scientific apparatus at the University of Maryland's Charged Particle Beam Laboratory, Jon Sutter fashions instruments that comment on high-tech society. He painted *Under Continuous Monitor* a gray green color commonly found on ubiquitous street furniture that designers want to make disappear—like electrical panels or telephone boxes. Yet, this piece demands attention because it sits atop a concrete block that gives it a sense of solidity and stability, similar to light poles and signposts. An anthropomorphic quality is seen in the "face" that comprises a clock, hygrometer, thermometer, and barometer.

But what, exactly, is under continuous monitor? Bluestone rocks, such as those used in road construction, fill the pedestal. The rocks are literally "under" the monitoring devices. Yet questions abound. Why monitor a pile of rocks? Who is at the other end of the transmitter receiving the information? And what does it all mean? Sutter wants viewers to find their own answers. He thinks of his work as a kind of poetry in which readers supply their own interpretation.[66] Sutter gave up his studio in Hagerstown, Maryland, to study full time at the Rhode Island School of Design.

[66] John Sutter, telephone interview with the author, August 8, 2005.

BAROMETER

BOB TROTMAN

born 1947
Winston-Salem, North Carolina

*Louise**

1997, limewood and maple with casters and rubber tread, 54 × 36 × 36. Gift of an anonymous donor and the Franklin Parrasch Gallery, New York, 1998.65

A 1969 GRADUATE OF WASHINGTON AND LEE University in Lexington, Virginia, with a degree in philosophy, Bob Trotman has worked in western North Carolina for thirty years. He taught himself furniture construction with a little help from a workshop led by Sam Maloof at the Penland School of Crafts in North Carolina in the 1970s. Trotman's pieces have evolved from functional furniture ornamented with figural carving, to figural carving with minimal function, to his present work, which is pure sculpture.

Louise is part of a series in which human figures seem trapped as pieces of furniture, creating a tension between our empathy for the carved figures and their "use" as furniture. Trotman drew his inspiration for his anthropomorphic sculptures from the fantastically carved misericord seats found in Romanesque cathedrals.[67] Bronze is the traditional material for sculpture, but Trotman likes the warmth and beauty of wood.

While *Louise,* carved from a laminated block of wood, functions effectively as library steps, it also makes a strong cultural statement. It is not a totally pessimistic idea, as Trotman is quick to say, even if the message is "a little dark."[68] *Louise,* the haggard office worker of the late 1940s and 1950s, is resigned to her fate of having the boss stand on her back as he advances in his career. In comparison, Trotman's earlier library steps of 1994, *Trust Me,* feature a crouching male grasping a staff, an image that suggests a more positive theme of Hercules supporting the world.

[67] Bob Trotman, telephone interview with the author, April 2004.

[68] Frances M. MacDougal, "Philosophical Furniture," *Southern Accents,* November–December 1995, 117.

UNION WOODWORKS

Andrew W. Palmer
John H. Norton
Michael A. Goldfinger
Christopher T. MacCarthy

Conference Table

1975, red oak and black walnut, 29 ½ × 120 × 42.
Museum purchase, 1975.179

ANDREW W. PALMER, JOHN H. NORTON, MICHAEL A. Goldfinger, and Christopher T. MacCarthy—all self-trained carpenters and woodworkers in their midtwenties—established a woodworking cooperative called Union Woodworks in an old Warren, Vermont, textile mill in 1971. When they read the announcement for the *Craft Multiples* show at the Renwick in 1975, they saw an opportunity to publicize their operation and possibly sell a piece of furniture. Palmer, who had worked in a furniture factory for a short time, designed the table and did most of the fabrication.[69] It was similar to a series of furniture the company was making for the University of Vermont at the time.

Once the table was assembled, the group decided that the pair of U-shaped legs supporting the top looked like two cowboys cut off at the waist. Goldfinger suggested they flip the base so the *U* stood upright, rather than downward, as originally conceived. The stretcher that connects the two supports originally ran directly under the tabletop, but when the supports were flipped, it was necessary to add a central leg support.

Through tenons penetrate the tabletop, and a small butterfly was inlaid into the surface to stop a potential check from spreading, a technique they knew from having studied the work of George Nakashima. In fact, they had visited the Nakashima compound in New Hope, Pennsylvania, as well as the nearby Wharton Esherick studio in Paoli.[70] A walnut accent strip runs down the middle of the table. Before an oil finish was applied, the eight-quarter oak top was machine-planed and hand-scraped, achieving a smoother surface than sanding would have given.

Although the company started out making one-of-a-kind residential furniture it sold through word of mouth or craft shows, Union Woodworks gradually moved into the field of commercial and institutional furniture. Now called WallGoldfinger Inc., the company has forty employees and specializes in high-end conference and boardroom tables.

[69] Michael A. Goldfinger, interview with the author, August 8, 2005.

[70] Ibid.

ROBERT WHITLEY

born 1924
Trenton, New Jersey

*Whitley Windsor Arm Chair**

1975, black walnut, 39 3/16 × 24 1/2 × 23 1/2. Museum purchase, 1975.180

COMING FROM A FAMILY OF FURNITURE MAKERS, Robert Whitley is a third-generation antique restorer and reproduction specialist working in Solebury, Pennsylvania. He has done extensive work for the National Park Service in Pennsylvania, and for one of his most prominent commissions, he reproduced John F. Kennedy's White House desk for the Kennedy Library in Massachusetts. Whitley made his first Windsor chair, a rocker for his wife, in 1951, when she was pregnant with their daughter.[71] He made this chair in 1975 for the *Craft Multiples* show at the Renwick Gallery, and it was among the museum's first acquisitions.

Basing the chair loosely on eighteenth-century, high-backed Windsors, Whitley squared off the crest and simplified the leg turnings, giving his interpretation sharp lines and a sleek modern look. He started with split spindles and then hand-shaped them with a spokeshave. Eighteenth-century Windsors were typically made with multiple woods such as pine for the seat, hickory or ash for the spindles, and maple for the legs. Like his Windsor rocker, however, Whitley constructed this chair completely from black walnut harvested on his property. Subsequent versions employed ash for the spindles and eliminated the U-shaped, continuous arm in favor of attaching two separate arms to the outermost spindles on the back.

[71] Robert Whitley, telephone interview with the author, April 16, 2004.

ROBERT WHITLEY

*Throne Chair**

1979, curly maple and walnut with ebony pegs, 34 ¼ × 35 × 25 ⅝.
Gift of Bradford McCormick, 1986.36

WHITLEY FOUND INSPIRATION FOR *THRONE CHAIR* in a massive Jacobean wainscot chair he saw on a visit to Edinburgh, Scotland.[72] Although the seventeenth-century oak chair was rectilinear in form, three hundred years of wear had softened its lines. His modern interpretation accentuates the soft edges of the original. Walnut pegs, used to secure the tenons, protrude on the front legs of *Throne Chair* and on the crest rail to mimic the protruding pegs on the old wainscot chair. The pegs protruded on the original because wood shrinks across the grain so the pegs shrink less than the surface of the legs. By combining light maple and dark walnut, Whitley broke up the lines of the chair and reduced its visual mass. *Throne Chair* resurrects the seventeenth-century idea that even domestic chairs could function as thrones, reserved for an honored guest or the revered head of the household. Whitley has expanded on the *Throne Chair* concept in a series of imposing desks, tables, and benches.

[72] Robert Whitley, telephone interview with the author, April 16, 2004.

ROB WOMACK

born 1957
Norfolk, Virginia

*All Sound**

2003, oil-based enamel on found French art deco sideboard with reverse painting on glass, 37 × 55 × 21½. Gift of Samuel G. Rose and Julie Walters in memory of Rudi Dornbusch, 2004.3a–b

THE STUDIO FURNITURE FIELD COMPRISES A VARIETY of makers. At one end of the continuum stand Tage Frid, George Nakashima, and Sam Maloof, who were primarily concerned with wood and technique. At the other end stands Rob Womack, who does not make furniture, but rather finds objects he can completely cover with paint. In *All Sound,* he bought a 1930s French art deco cabinet on eBay. To provide an uninterrupted canvas for his painting, he replaced the feet and the glass top and removed the pulls. Womack then stripped the walnut case, filled the worm holes, and repainted it with numerous base coats of enamel. He sketched the cityscape on tracing paper, transferred the image to the surface of the cabinet, and painted the final picture.[73] Womack's painting skill reveals his fine art training at Virginia Commonwealth University in Richmond, where he now resides and works.

As Womack researched an appropriate scene that would complement the style of the cabinet, he came across a series of photographs documenting construction of the Chrysler Building in New York City in the late 1920s. In the background stood a theater whose marquee advertised "All Sound," a reference to the newly popular talking movies of the era. The title also evokes the many sounds of a busy city, an idea that contrasts with Womack's typical unpeopled and silent tableau. With the carefully researched color palette and the angular jazz-age composition, Womack has captured the spirit of the period.

[73] Rob Womack, telephone interview with the author, April 2004.

RICK WRIGLEY

born 1955
Arlington, Virginia

The Rick Wrigley Renwick Cabinet

2001, Honduran mahogany, ebony, maple, anigré, pomelé sapelé, marquetry veneers (Australian walnut, holly, various maples, lemonwood, pearwood, East Indian rosewood, and cow bone), medium-density fiberboard, Negro marquina marble, and brass, 40 × 46 × 22. Gift of the James Renwick Alliance, 2001.37

RICK WRIGLEY LEARNED THE FUNDAMENTALS OF cabinetmaking as an apprentice after high school and earned his degree from the School for American Craftsmen at the Rochester Institute of Technology, where he refined his technique and design sense. His studio is now located in Provincetown, Massachusetts.

Wrigley made the first of three sideboards in this series for the *New American Furniture* exhibition at the Museum of Fine Arts, Boston in 1989.[74] He based the design on a sideboard by William Hook of Salem, Massachusetts, about 1808–1809. With Wrigley's intense study of American furniture makers such as Duncan Phyfe and Charles-Honoré Lannuier from the early nineteenth century, it is not surprising his entry in the show was the closest in appearance to the period object that served as his inspiration.[75]

Disappointed at missing the opportunity to acquire the *New American Furniture* piece, the Renwick Alliance commissioned Wrigley to make a similar sideboard. For the Renwick, he decided to simplify the original design and was even happier with the more unified result.[76] While his first attempt set off the wedges making up the fan on the façade with dark mahogany banding, the wedges on *The Rick Wrigley Renwick Cabinet* are only subtly differentiated by a slight change in color. The piece's inlaid, four-point spires behind the planished brass knobs substitute for patinated copper discs on the piece from the Boston show.[77] Wrigley also eliminated the nail heads that outlined the base on the first design and replaced the granite on the top with black marble that appears less modern. In the Renwick cabinet, the eagles grasping snakes in their beaks symbolize the eternal battle between good and evil. That motif, surrounded by olive leaves and branches, substituted for the first cabinet's inlay design—figures holding banners and a band of inlaid blocks based on floor designs in the cathedral of Siena, Italy.

---

[74] Cooke, *New American Furniture*, 124–127.

[75] Ibid., 124.

[76] Rick Wrigley, telephone interview with the author, April 2004.

[77] To planish is to polish by hammering.

A Statistical Snapshot of the Collection

THE STUDIO FURNITURE FIELD MAY INCLUDE MORE THAN twenty thousand cabinetmakers across the country.[1] As the nation's showcase of craft in all media, the Renwick Gallery has sought to collect representative samples of that vast body of work. To that end, a succession of three curators has acquired eighty-four pieces of furniture by sixty-four artists. Some forty of those makers were surveyed in the author's 2005 article about the one hundred most influential cabinetmakers published in *Furniture Studio 3*.[2]

The *Furniture Studio* article presented a snapshot of the field based on data gathered from telephone interviews with the makers. The surveys elicited basic biographical data, information about shop practices, marketing strategies, aesthetic influences, design approaches, and opinions on trends in the field. A similar methodology was employed with those represented in the Renwick collection to develop a picture of the group.[3] The goal was to compare research on the Renwick artists with similar research describing the top makers in the field and to add to the understanding of studio furniture makers and their methods.

In many respects, the Renwick sample gives a broader sense of the field than the previous survey. An important difference is the Renwick collection features a significant number of midcareer artists. While the earlier survey studied only established makers as defined largely by their degree of notoriety, the Renwick collection represents the subjective judgments of the curators who amassed the collection. The majority of the work that Lloyd Herman added to the collection came from submissions by young cabinetmakers to the *Craft Multiples* exhibition. Because Michael Monroe added a number of canonical pieces to the collection, Ken Trapp probably felt free to collect lesser-known makers along with established names.

Additionally, the Renwick collection includes categories of pieces that were outside the scope of the earlier survey. Three makers in the Renwick collection—Jacob Cress, John Higginbotham, and Robert Whitley—create fine reproductions, a category excluded from the *Furniture Studio* study. The industrial design category also was not considered in the earlier article, but that group is represented in the Renwick collection by Peter Danko. The Renwick even contains an early twentieth-century chest from the Byrdcliffe arts-and-crafts community that predates the studio furniture movement. And finally, artists who occasionally create furniture but do not focus on the field were absent from the *Furniture Studio* study. In the Renwick collection, fiber artist Norma Minkowitz falls into that category. In short, the Renwick's diverse collection represents a broader view of the field—and presents different insights—than the subjects of the earlier study.

BIOGRAPHICAL FINDINGS | MORE THAN FIFTY YEARS AGO, when several of the first generation started making furniture, people tended to chose a career for life. In recent times, however, workers have been more likely to change careers, and the furniture field has not been immune to the trend.

Of the makers represented in the Renwick collection, six have left the field for more lucrative employment: Richard Ford, Joanne Shima, John Higginbotham, Paul Buckley, Richard John, and Rory McCarthy. Bob Trotman gave up furniture making to become a full-time sculptor.

Jenna Goldberg, *Falling Leaves* (detail); see page 99.

On the other hand, two became cabinetmakers later in life. Steve Perrin abandoned a graphic design career in his early forties to become a furniture maker, and Robert Bliss took up the craft at age sixty-five, after he retired from a career in architecture.

About 40 percent of respondents had at least short careers in other fields before becoming cabinetmakers. John Higginbotham and Michael Hurwitz made musical instruments. Michael Sterling was a nurse; Stephen Courtney, a photographer; Daniel Mack, a journalist; and Dave Merrifield and Charles Radtke were engineers. Albert Paley and Garry Knox Bennett began by making jewelry. For some, these earlier careers continue to provide income so they can pursue at least part time their passion for furniture making.

Now in their eighties, only Robert Whitley and Evert Sodergren have retired after long furniture-making careers. Of the five craftsmen who have died: Art Carpenter, Tage Frid, George Nakashima, Dan Jackson, and Wharton Esherick, all worked up until their death or, in the case of Jackson, until illness forced him to stop working.[4]

The respondents ranged in age from Dave Chapman, Dave Merrifield, and Jenna Goldberg—all thirty-nine years old—to Sam Maloof at ninety-one. Inexplicably, only five, or fewer than 10 percent, were women, a marked contrast to 17 percent in the larger survey. More than half were in their forties and fifties, and eight were in their sixties. Of the ten makers aged over eighty, Sam Maloof and Robert Bliss are still working. Randy Shull started selling furniture professionally at age fifteen, but the majority (57 percent) began their careers in their twenties, most of them soon after college. With the exception of two men who made career changes later in life, the rest began selling their furniture professionally in their thirties. These respondents typically delayed beginning their careers to complete a graduate degree or had started another career for a short period and needed time for self training.

Makers represented in the Renwick collection lived most frequently in Massachusetts (fourteen), California (ten), New York (seven), Pennsylvania (five), and Rhode Island (four), with the remaining 39 percent scattered across the country in twelve different states and in Vancouver, British Columbia. Many seem to congregate in the four states where the major craft schools are located: in New York with the Rochester Institute of Technology (RIT), in California with the programs at San Diego State and the California College of the Arts (formerly the California College of Arts and Crafts), in Pennsylvania with the Pennsylvania College of Arts, and in Rhode Island with the Rhode Island School of Design (RISD).

A surprising 52 percent of the artists in the Renwick collection are self-taught woodworkers, compared to only 28 percent in the major maker survey. About half of these already had a background either in architecture or fine art, so they only had to master the technical skills before launching studio furniture careers. No doubt because of their primary interest in wood and technique, about half of the self-trained cabinetmakers fall into the category of first generation or first-generation interpreters. The remainder take a more artistic approach they developed largely on a trial-and-error basis. Of the eighteen makers with bachelor or master's degrees in fine arts, all graduated from one of the three major furniture programs: seven from the Program in Artisanry at Boston University, seven from the Rochester Institute of Technology, and four from the Rhode Island School of Design.

In addition to formal degree programs in furniture design, a number of the cabinetmakers entered the field with other educational experience. Six of them trained as fine artists including Norma Minkowitz, Shinichi Miyazaki, Albert Paley, Tommy Simpson, Roy Superior, and Robert Womack. Three others held architecture degrees—Robert Bliss, George Nakashima, and Peter Pittman. John Eric Byers and Peter Pierobon attended the Wendell Castle School in the 1980s, before it closed in 1988. Christina Madsen received her training at the Leeds Design Workshop in Easthampton, Massachusetts, which was established by Englishman David Powell in the 1970s. Ken Schmahmann graduated from the North Bennet Street School in Boston.

Earning a living as a full-time cabinetmaker is difficult. Of the Renwick artists, 37 percent worked part time, commonly augmenting their income with such occupations as antique restoration, product design, interior remodeling, contracting, and especially teaching. In fact, about 20 percent of the Renwick's cabinetmakers taught on a regular basis. Even full-time makers sought short-term teaching positions in non-degree programs at the Penland School of Crafts in North Carolina, Anderson Ranch Art Center in Colorado, the Haystack Mountain School of Crafts in Maine, the Appalachian Center for Crafts, and the Arrowmont School of Arts and Crafts, both in Tennessee. While teaching had its rewards, for most in the field, it was the act of creating that energized them. Teaching merely funded that passion.

In the earlier survey of the most influential furniture makers, only 40 percent worked full time in the shop. However, in the Renwick sample, 63 percent of the makers worked full time in their studios. Perhaps explaining the discrepancy, the most established makers tended to have more teaching opportunities and thus considered their studio work part time. Midcareer artists, which make up about half of the Renwick collection, had varied work patterns.[5] Some focused on furniture making full time in order to participate in craft shows, which is where Ken Trapp saw the work of many midcareer artists he later acquired for the collection. Of course, the very top makers were also able to work in their studios full time, but they typically sold through high-end galleries, not through craft shows.

SHOP PRACTICES | INFLUENCED BY WILLIAM MORRIS AND the arts-and-crafts movement in the late nineteenth century, the public usually believes the myth that furniture makers, at least since the Middle Ages, enjoyed the satisfaction of fabricating their own designs. According to critics, that happy arrangement changed in the nineteenth century with the Industrial Revolution. At that time, the designer and the cabinetmaker's tasks were separated, and the latter was reduced to functioning like a robot on an assembly line, making only one small part of a larger product. Although in reality, craftsmen rarely had the luxury of producing whatever they wanted, the myth of the designer-craftsman took hold and actually became a reality beginning with Wharton Esherick in the early twentieth century. Regarded as the founder of the studio furniture movement, Esherick was the first nationally known figure to make a living selling his own designs, but even he had assistants help him fabricate furniture in his shop.

Only about 41 percent of the makers (as opposed to about half in the study on influential makers) fit the stereotype of the cabinetmaker toiling alone in a small shop—and even these solitary workers on occasion relied on spouses or shop assistants to help with heavy lifting. Another 40 percent had from one to three assistants. Eight makers worked with four to ten craftsmen. Four—George Nakashima, Peter Danko, Albert Paley, and Evert Sodergren— ran small production shops that employed more than ten journeymen in their heyday. One-third of the cabinetmakers contracted out some of their work, including finishing, carving, turning, bronze casting and other metal work, and sometimes upholstery. The operations require specialized equipment and space, luxuries for small cabinet shops. In some cases, makers with large commissions contracted for multiple legs for a set of chairs or other repetitive tasks that do not require design decisions.

Virtually all of the artisans began the design process with sketches. One, however, Tom Loeser, has started using a digital camera to record images that might lead to design ideas rather than taking the time to sketch them. About a third used models or mockups to help them work out complicated designs, though sometimes they used models as a means to help the client visualize the commission. While the majority of the makers produced full shop drawings from their sketches, about 40 percent said their work evolved as they made it. The eight makers—including Garry Knox Bennett, John Eric Byers, Randy Shull, and Roy Superior—who proceeded directly from sketches to fabrication, usually produced work that required less complicated joinery. About an equal number, such as Jenna Goldberg, Timothy Philbrick, and Roseanne Somerson, adhered closely to detailed shop drawings, particularly if the piece was complex and involved contractors or apprentices. Many makers, such as John Cederquist and Sam Maloof, explained that as they gained experience, they relied less and less on full-scale drawings and allowed the design to evolve during the fabrication process. Their goal was to achieve a sense of spontaneity and looseness in the design.

Ten makers admitted to using the computer to do the shop drawings or to create three-dimensional models. At 16 percent, this is the same ratio found in the sample of influential makers. Computer design is a necessity for those using computer-controlled tools such as Dale Broholm, who employed a computer-controlled laser to cut intricate inlay. Other makers, however, feared the computer would erase the mark of the hand from their work. For the first generation and first-generation interpreters, using a computer is considered heresy. But the younger generation, having grown up with computers, see them as just another tool—and one that can do more complex work. The Renwick collection does not contain any good examples of pieces that take advantage of the computer to generate complex designs. That no doubt reflects the curators' lack of focus on the issue and the fact that only recently have computerized tools made significant inroads into the studio furniture field.

Output varied considerably depending upon the size of the shop, but also upon gallery commitments and number of commissions. On average, two-thirds of the furniture makers produced one or two pieces per month. Two craftsmen known for their chairs, Sam Maloof and Robert Erickson, turned out five to ten pieces per month with the help of several assistants. Robert Whitley completed about five chairs a month but also ran an antique restoration and reproduction business. Evert Sodergren (now retired) achieved a similar output, but many of his pieces were more complex Japanese style *tansu* chests, which are usually more complex than chairs. When Peter Danko made the furniture now in the Renwick collection, he operated a small furniture factory where he employed twenty-five workers and recorded an annual output of three thousand to four thousand chairs a year. George Nakashima managed a smaller operation, with twelve people producing five hundred to six hundred pieces a year. At the other extreme is Kim Schmahmann, whose work is so complex he finishes only one piece every few years.

In the studio furniture field, rarity certainly influences the value of a piece. The more complex and longer it takes to make an object, the fewer are made. Paradoxically, however, the secondary market for George Nakashima's work has been stronger than for virtually any other maker in part because his output was relatively large. The result is collectors have a good chance of acquiring his work. On the other hand, Wharton Esherick is arguably a more important maker, but his output was so small his work rarely comes up for auction. He has a more limited following. A craftsperson's output, therefore, can influence demand and value, but not always in predictable patterns.

While half the makers produced the whole range of furniture forms, another third preferred to make mostly chairs. Chairs are probably the most challenging furniture form. Simultaneously, chairs are a necessity that find a ready market. Even so, five makers favored producing cabinets, and an equal number specialized in tables and desks. Sixty percent of the makers produced only one-of-a-kind furniture, while eight makers—notably Peter Danko, George Nakashima, Robert Whitley, and Evert Sodergren—produced limited editions. Wendell Castle continues to produce one-of-a-kind pieces, but he recently established a small manufacturing company as well. David Ebner and Judy McKie cast multiples of some of their furniture in bronze, partly to save the backbreaking labor of producing the same pieces over and over in wood. Experts often disagree about when a one-of-a-kind object becomes a production run. A rule of thumb limits studio furniture to a dozen, and each must reflect some aspect of the maker's hand. Under that definition, Peter Danko's *Unfolding Chair* would be considered a production piece, as would George Nakashima's *Lounge Chair,* both of which were produced by the thousands.

MARKETING STRATEGIES | SOMETIMES SELLING THE furniture proves to be a more difficult challenge than making it. The division between commission and speculative work mirrors the results of the previous survey of the most influential makers. About 54 percent executed all or mostly commissions, while 33 percent produced work largely on speculation, primarily for galleries. Some 12 percent split their work evenly between the two approaches.

Even though 84 percent of the respondents confirmed they had exhibited in galleries at some time in their careers, the trend among the Renwick group seemed to involve producing more work on commission for individual clients and creating fewer speculative pieces for sale in galleries. In the short run, the strategy increased the income of the maker, who avoided gallery commissions of up to 50 percent. However, in the long term, as galleries have disappeared, artists have not been promoted and demand has diminished. Several years ago, the John Elder Gallery in New York City closed. Only about half a dozen galleries, which focus on furniture at the highest price point, remain, including Leo Kaplan Modern in New York City; Lewis

Wexler in Philadelphia; Tercera in San Francisco; and Pritam & Eames in East Hampton, Long Island. The halcyon days of the late 1980s and 1990s, when the Peter Joseph Gallery in New York City created a buzz in the field and even paid retainers to struggling makers, seem gone forever.

As an alternative to selling though galleries, about half of the makers have exhibited in craft shows at least once in their career. Shows and sponsors included the American Craft Council, the *Smithsonian Craft Show*, and the *Philadelphia Furniture and Furnishings Show*. For one-quarter of those who entered craft shows early in their career, once or twice was enough, and they quickly turned to other sales outlets. Craft shows are grueling, not only from the standpoint of having to make a body of furniture to display, but also because of the physical demands of setting up and manning the booth for four or five days at a time. For the best-known makers, the craft show circuit is not necessary because they already have enough business. In some cases, established makers have teaching responsibilities that render a show's schedule impossible. However, for makers starting out, craft shows are a traditional avenue of entry. They offer some makers a marketing strategy to gain exposure. Because of the time required to prepare for and attend a craft show, the majority of those who exhibit are full-time cabinetmakers.

Only about one-quarter of the respondents had showrooms or even encouraged customers to see furniture in their homes or shops. Dangerous and often cramped, workshops are not conducive to walk-in traffic, and many makers did not want the constant interruption. An increasingly popular alternative is the Internet. More than 65 percent of the makers maintained Web sites, as compared with only 40 percent in the survey conducted a year earlier. The Internet, as a sales tool for makers, is definitely catching on. No doubt many artists see the Web as a way to bypass gallery commissions. Via the Internet, interested customers can view work rather than journeying to often remote workshops where only current work can be seen. On the other hand, many makers recognized Web sites cannot replace personal interaction with customers and the tactile experience of the furniture, both of which are important to most prospective clients. In addition, the Web has not generated the same excitement and sizzle galleries produce. Thus, while the Internet may be broadening the audience for craft, the potential customers might not be as passionate as earlier clients who typically made purchases through galleries.

APPROACHES | ALTHOUGH AT FIRST GLANCE EACH PIECE OF furniture in the collection appears unrelated, a closer inspection reveals similarities that make it possible to group the artworks around specific approaches. In short, the Renwick's furniture can be divided into eight different categories depending upon the primary emphasis. The first three groups are fairly straightforward—pieces made by the first generation, those created by first-generation interpreters, and reproductions. The final five are derived from the second generation's emphasis on narrative elements, whimsy, surface decoration, nontraditional materials, and sculpture.[6] Although some artworks embody several approaches, the maker's primary focus is usually clear. For example, Jenna Goldberg explained her work carries subtle messages, but the focus of her cabinets is obviously the lavish surface decoration of both the interior and exterior. In the case of three makers—Peter Danko, Wendell Castle, and John Cederquist—the collection contains works from different stages of their careers, representing different approaches.

For the first generation of makers (seven in the collection), there was no question about their focus. Their work was about wood, techniques, and the process of making. All were heavily influenced by eighteenth-century Windsor chairs, Shaker simplicity, and Scandinavian design, which became popular in the 1950s. By definition, these were the first makers to earn a living selling their work to a wide public. While Wharton Esherick, the patriarch of this generation, began his career in the 1920s, most of the rest began working in the 1940s and 1950s. Sam Maloof is still working today.

Tage Frid, first at the Rochester Institute of Technology and then at the Rhode Island School of Design, taught the first-generation values—that technique comes first and should determine design—to a rising group of young makers. Many of his students, such as John Dunnigan, Jere Osgood, and Daniel Jackson, interpreted the tradition in their own work and have passed the precepts on to another generation through their teaching. In addition to the educators, notables in the first-generation interpreters category include David Ebner, Charles Radtke, and Robert Erickson. Altogether about 33 percent of those in the Renwick collection fall into the first generation or first-generation interpreters categories.

Three craftsmen—John Higginbotham, Timothy Philbrick, and Rick Wrigley—made adaptations or close copies of eighteenth- and early nineteenth-century American furniture. Michael Sterling reproduced a chair from the arts-and-crafts movement in the early twentieth century. Like the first generation, the four makers emphasized wood and technique, but they also added a reverence for traditional American furniture design. Much of the work by John Dunnigan could fall into the same category. In the case of his *Slipper Chairs*, however, the strong autobiographical references clearly consign them to the narrative category.

The proper classification of furniture, particularly among second-generation makers, is not always clear. Depending upon what elements are emphasized, furniture can fall into several different categories. Kim Schmahmann was trained in a historical furniture tradition at the North Bennet Street School. Nevertheless, his *Bureau of Bureaucracy*, while based on traditional cabinet forms, is primarily a narrative, really a political commentary. Schmahmann falls into the second generation of makers whose interest in storytelling takes their work beyond fine craftsmanship and wood. Twenty-three percent of the artists in the Renwick's collection share a narrative approach.

Although Tommy Simpson has called his work whimsical, and it could be included in the whimsical category, his personal narrative content was even stronger. A sense of humor informs the work of Jacob Cress, who became bored with standard reproductions that allow very little design creativity. Like Bennett's 1979 *Nail Cabinet*, which protested slavish attention to technique, Cress's *Oops!* chair implies furniture should do more than just demonstrate superior technique; it should tell a funny story. Humor is the principal goal of four of the pieces in the Renwick, including Craig Nutt's vegetable confection, Richard Ford's cartoon vanity, and Joanne Shima's child's chair.

About 10 percent of the cabinetmakers eschew wood altogether or use it in conjunction with other materials. The challenge for them is to make furniture with nontraditional materials, particularly metal. Albert

Paley is the best-known name in that group. David Chapman worked in willow, and Robert Bliss used a selection of materials besides wood to achieve his designs. Danko used wood, but it was modern plywood he pressed into unlikely shapes. Bennett, the consummate artist, took wood and a variety of man-made materials and combined them into a unified whole in his *Boston Kneehole*.

Sometimes artists emphasize the surface of the material—rather than the media itself—when they approach it as a canvas to decorate. Four makers in the Renwick collection fall into this category: John Eric Byers, Tom Loeser, Jenna Goldberg, and Kristina Madsen. Although Byers and Loeser think of their work as sculpture, which it is, the untold hours they invest in painting the surface really becomes their main focus. Similarly, Madsen expends the same extraordinary effort in decorating her surfaces with carving.

All furniture has three-dimensional shape and thus is sculptural, but some of the objects in the Renwick (nearly 17 percent) focus on that attribute primarily. While Peter Pierobon's *Time Totem* has a narrative component, it is principally about the interplay of shapes and is thus sculptural. John Dunnigan pointed out that although his chairs are a study in shape and form, they impart a strong narrative content. The wall cabinet by John Cederquist and the desk by Wendell Castle clearly belong in the sculptural category, but Castle's *Ghost Clock* and all of Cederquist's later trompe l'oeil work fall into the narrative group. While sculpture and narrative categories can overlap, if a piece had a clear narrative message, it was put into that category.

Whatever the approach, almost 80 percent avoid social or political statements in their furniture. The majority of the work that focuses on wood and technique (the first generation and first generation interpreters), on form (as in the sculptural group), and on surface and materials, does not readily lend itself to social commentary. An exception was Peter Danko, who focused on material to promote environmentally friendly furniture long before that cause became fashionable. Still, of the fifteen makers who espouse a gender or political message, half took the narrative approach. The best examples are Daniel Mack and Peter Pittman, who used found objects to passionately convey ethnic, political, and even religious messages. Most, however, wanted their furniture to make a positive statement in order to appeal to a wide audience, rather than to appear polarizing or polemical. Broad political statements might be suitable for museum pieces that will be seen by many people, but most furniture is purchased by individuals—often as a personal commission. In that sense, studio furniture frequently spurs a private dialogue between the artist and the client.

AESTHETIC INFLUENCES | WHATEVER THE EMPHASIS—FIRST generation, first-generation interpreter, adaptations, narrative, material, surface, sculpture, or whimsy—all the cabinetmakers have been influenced to one degree or another by either modern art or historical furniture styles. Only three makers—fiber artist Norma Minkowitz, fine artist Roy Superior, and Jenna Goldberg, all of whom are interested primarily in surface design—claimed no historical furniture influences. Although Goldberg holds a fine art degree, she drew her inspiration primarily from decorative arts objects.

In America, the eighteenth and early nineteenth centuries are considered the golden age of furniture making, so it is not surprising this era exerted the largest impact with eighteen mentions in the survey. If Shaker furniture at fifteen mentions and arts-and-crafts furniture at eight are included, more than 80 percent of the makers owed a debt to the work of traditional American cabinetmakers. All of the respondents appreciated the extraordinary technical virtuosity exhibited routinely by their forebears. Reflecting an understandable nativism, only ten makers cited antique European furniture, mostly French, as an inspiration, while eight acknowledged ancient Egyptian and Greek antecedents for all the period and revival styles.

Because the studio furniture movement had its roots in the 1950s when the popularity of Scandinavian design peaked, it is logical that more than one-third of the makers cited it as a major inspiration. Hans Wegner, the Danish designer, along with Alvar Aalto of Finland, and Charles and Ray Eames in the United States were singled out. Asian, especially Japanese, design was the next most influential, touching about one-third of the makers. The simple lines and tradition of fine craftsmanship that were the hallmarks of Scandinavian design are also present in Asian design, which influenced one-third of the makers. Japanese influence is most evident in the trompe l'oeil work of John Cederquist and more subtly in the furniture of Michael Hurwitz and Thomas Hucker.

The rich woods and the fine craftsmanship of 1920s and 1930s art deco furniture moved some 20 percent of respondents to acknowledge their debt to that style. The exotic woods in Rainer Facklam's cabinet and the streamlined form of John Cederquist's wall cabinet best illustrate the art deco influence in the collection. African art, a component of the art deco style, was cited as an influence by almost the same number. Cabinetmakers identified as influential other exotic cultures, such as Polynesian, Celtic, pre-Columbian, and Northwest Coast and American Indian.

Despite the preponderant impact of Scandinavian, Asian, and art deco design, a significant number (eleven) pointed to the high-tech designs of the German Bauhaus as an important source for their work. Artists highlighted the furniture of Mies van der Rohe and Marcel Breuer, who were associated with the German Bauhaus along with their French contemporaries Le Corbusier and his partners, Charlotte Perriand and Pierre Jeanneret.

The ornate creations of art nouveau designers exerted almost as much sway as the Bauhaus with eight mentions. The early twentieth-century work of Antonio Gaudí in Spain, Garrit Rietveld and the de Stijl in Holland, and Charles Rennie Mackintosh in Scotland earned special mentions. The flowing steel ribbons of Albert Paley's *Lectern* epitomize the art nouveau influence.

Sixteen makers denied any trace of modern art in their work (about 20 percent of the total). Only two in the group attended formal art schools where they might have been exposed to contemporary art. Most of the group fell into the categories of first generation or first-generation interpreters, which looked largely to past furniture styles for inspiration rather than to fine art.

However, for the remaining 80 percent of the cabinetmakers in the Renwick collection, a range of artists and modern art movements were mentioned as influencing their work. Surrealist artists René Magritte and Salvador Dalí were singled out. The minimalist sculpture of Donald Judd and abstract work by Constantin Brancusi, Jean Arp, and Henry Moore exerted an obvious impact on sculptors such as Garry Knox Bennett and Wendell Castle. The effect of the readymades of Marcel Duchamp, and later pop art, can be seen in the work of Craig Nutt and Daniel Mack. Wharton Esherick's work, both his sculpture and his furniture, is clearly informed by the cubism of Pablo Picasso and Georges Braque, which was just emerging when he was in art school in Philadelphia.

By far, the largest influence was post modernism, which hit the art world in the 1970s, just as the studio furniture movement was gaining momentum. Indeed, Alphonse Mattia credited post modernism with showing him alternatives to the first-generation approach and encouraging him to experiment with color and different materials. At the same time, post modernism led John Dunnigan to reject modernism altogether and return to traditional furniture design. More specifically, the precariously perched hatboxes of John Eric Byers clearly espouse the post-modern belief in the instability and evanescent nature of the modern world.

Many respondents expressed the belief that no new design movement had yet arisen to challenge post modernism. Judy McKie observed there has been a traditional cycle between ornament and simplicity. Simplicity was followed by the era of ornament in post-modern design, and she saw a trend toward simplicity emerging again today. Others felt design had become much too personal and narcissistic and risked losing its universal appeal. Some said designs are striving to be different just for the sake of difference, and have lost their meaning. Tommy Simpson seemed to have transcended that pitfall. Although his furniture has very personal, often autobiographical content, it also has universal appeal. If there were any agreement on the state of design today it was summed up in the word *eclectic*.

Although roughly half the makers in the Renwick collection traveled outside the United States at one time or another, at least five stated travel had very little impact on their work. Some, such as Jon Sutter, said traveling within the United States had influenced their work more than travel in Europe. Asia and South America topped the list of continents visited, but Scandinavia exerted a disproportionate influence. The furniture of Jere Osgood, Dan Jackson, and Robert Erickson shows the direct impact of their sojourns there. Tage Frid, who was born in Denmark, trained a whole generation of studio furniture makers in the Scandinavian tradition. Although seven makers had visited Japan (Miyazaki was born there), the work of George Nakashima, Thomas Hucker, and Michael Hurwitz revealed the Japanese aesthetic most clearly in the simplicity of their designs and in their reverence for wood. Hurwitz and Randy Shull also spent time in Altos de Chavon, an artist colony in the Dominican Republic, where they developed a heightened sense of color. The Maori-inspired carving by Kristina Madsen represents the most direct influence of travel on any of the studio furniture in the Renwick.

Echoing society's increasing concern for the environment, Peter Danko has become a strong advocate for green design in furniture. By using plywood and recycled materials, he has demonstrated a substantial amount of wood and other natural materials can be saved. He believed young people were more open to environmentally friendly ideas, including new and different materials. Stephen Courtney and Charles Radtke echoed these sentiments in their selection of wood from renewable forests.

TRENDS IN THE FIELD | IS THE FIELD OF STUDIO FURNITURE getting bigger and prospering? When asked that question, about 30 percent of respondents had no opinion, reflecting the fact that many of them work in isolation and have no sense of what the rest of the field is doing. Of those who did express an opinion, 57 percent believed the field was expanding, a slightly larger majority than expressed by makers in the earlier survey. Interestingly, of the makers who had retired, half thought the field was expanding. At least seven makers, including some teachers at the major schools such as RIT and RISD, identified a trend away from personally making furniture and into industrial design or pure art and sculpture. Alphonse Mattia at RISD estimated that perhaps two-thirds of his graduates were choosing industrial design rather than solitary studio furniture work. He observed that this generation is not enamored with the romantic, counterculture notion from the 1970s of furniture makers toiling away in their shops and living on a pittance.

Several observed that because of the popularity of industrial design, the studio furniture field is not attracting as much new blood. Many thought the halcyon days of the movement in the 1980s and early 1990s had passed and the field has plateaued. Some lamented the shrinkage in the number of galleries. At the same time, others observed more schools, museums, conferences, publications, and other organizations, such as the Furniture Society, are promoting studio furniture than ever before.

Looking back on a successful half-century career in the studio furniture field, Evert Sodergren perhaps best summed up the state of the field when he said there was more interest in studio furniture now than fifty years ago, and with the higher standard of living today, more customers can afford to buy studio furniture. Still in the prime of his career, Charles Radtke echoed these sentiments when he stated, "As the Baby Boomer generation gets older, they want to have personal, intimate objects that challenge convention in their lives. They are more open-minded than the conservative generation of the 1950s."

The statistical analysis confirms the Renwick studio furniture collection admirably showcases both canonical makers as well as lesser-known and midcareer artists. It also reveals some of the gaps inevitable in any collection. Although the Renwick includes work by an impressive two-thirds of the most important makers, a few names are conspicuously absent. The addition of work by Wendy Maruyama, for example, would acknowledge one of the most creative and influential second-generation makers and also help to redress the underrepresentation of women in the collection. Although the first generation of makers is remarkably well showcased, an example by James Krenov, whose work and writings touched a whole generation of craftsmen, would help to complete that story. More midcareer artists such as Andy Buck, who teaches at the Rochester Institute of Technology, deserve consideration. And finally as the craft field enters the computer age, it is increasingly important to document the amazing versatility of this new tool through furniture by such makers as Rich Tannen, who teaches the next generation of furniture makers at the Rochester Institute of Technology.

Notes

[1] This figure is based on estimates by John Kelsey, longtime editor and writer in the studio furniture field and editor of *Furniture Studio*, the journal of the Furniture Society. The society has about 2,000 dues-paying members, but Kelsey and the society believe there are more than ten times that number working at least part time as studio furniture makers.

[2] Oscar P. Fitzgerald, "The Movers & Shakers & How They Got There." *Furniture Studio 3* (Free Union, VA: The Furniture Society, 2005) pp. 92–105. The preliminary list of the 109 most influential makers was developed by Charlene Johnson based on a survey of 105 craft publications as an independent study project in the author's spring 2004 History of Studio Furniture class, part of the Smithsonian Institution/Parsons School of Design master's program in the decorative arts.

[3] Students in the author's spring 2003 Smithsonian/Parsons class in American Studio Furniture—Christian Chute, Marcee Craighill, Samira Farmer, Kate Hughes, Pam Licht, Kate Livie, April Pride, and Virginia Waring—completed fourteen of the telephone interviews. Betsy Davison completed seven of the interviews as part of the spring 2005 Smithsonian Institution/Parsons class in Twentieth-Century Studio Furniture. The author completed forty interviews during a Renwick Fellowship between April and September 2005. Richard John and Christopher Sabin, artists who had submitted work for the Renwick's *Craft Multiples* exhibition in 1975, could not be located. Transcripts of these interviews are stored in the accession files of the Renwick Gallery and in the Smithsonian's Archives of American Art.

[4] In the case of four of the deceased makers, the author completed the questionnaires using published sources. Art Carpenter was interviewed prior to his death. The author is grateful to Mira Nakashima for providing information about her father, George Nakashima, and to Rosanne Somerson and John Dunnigan for information about Tage Frid, who had been their teacher.

[5] See the essay "Building the Collection" (pages 22–24) for a full definition and description of midcareer makers and the artworks acquired by Kenneth Trapp.

[6] The Renwick Gallery's 2004 *Right At Home* exhibition of its studio furniture collection curated by Ken Trapp grouped the pieces in the following categories: color and finish, form and function, metal and fiber, sculpture, and new classicism.

Bibliography

OVERVIEWS

Boyd, Virginia T. and Glenn Adamson. *Contemporary Studio Case Furniture: The Inside Story*. Madison, WI: Elvehjem Museum of Art, 2002.

Conway, Patricia. *Art for Everyday: The New Craft Movement*. New York: Clarkson Potter Publishers, 1990.

Cooke Jr., Edward S., Gerald W. R. Ward, and Kelly H. L'Ecuyer. *The Maker's Hand: American Studio Furniture 1940–1990*. Boston: MFA Publications, 2003.

Cooke Jr., Edward S. *New American Furniture: The Second Generation of Studio Furnituremakers*. Boston: Museum of Fine Arts, 1989.

Hosaluk, Michael. *Scratching the Surface: Art and Content in Contemporary Wood*. Madison, WI: Guild Publishing, 2002.

Plotnicov, Miriam Davidson. *Craft Multiples*. Washington, DC: Smithsonian Institution Press, 1975.

Smith, Paul J. and Edward Lucie-Smith. *Craft Today: Poetry of the Physical*. New York: Weidenfeld & Nicolson, 1986.

Trapp, Kenneth R. *Masters of Their Craft: Highlights from the Smithsonian American Art Museum*. Washington, DC: Smithsonian American Art Museum, 2003.

Trapp, Kenneth R. and Howard Risatti. *Skilled Work: American Craft at the Renwick Gallery*. Washington, DC: Smithsonian Institution Press, 1998.

GARRY KNOX BENNETT

Bellevue Arts Museum. *Garry Knox Bennett: Call Me Chairmaker*. Bellevue, WA: Bellevue Arts Museum, 2006.

Ilse-Neuman, Ursula, Arthur C. Danto, and Edward S. Cooke Jr. *Made in Oakland: The Furniture of Garry Knox Bennett*. New York: American Craft Museum, 2001.

Jones, Harvey L. *California Woodworking*. Oakland: Oakland Museum of Art, 1980.

Joseph, Peter T. *Garry Knox Bennett in Oakland*. New York: Peter Joseph Gallery, 1993.

Kelsey, John. "Portfolio: Garry Knox Bennett." *Fine Woodworking*, no. 45 (March–April 1984): 79–81.

Stone, Michael A. *Contemporary American Woodworkers*. Salt Lake City, UT: Peregrine Smith Books, 1986.

———. "Gary Knox Bennett." *American Craft* 44, no. 5 (October–November 1984): 22–26.

———. "Profile: Garry Knox Bennett." *Woodwork*, no. 71 (October 2001): 24–30.

White, Cheryl. "Garry Knox Bennett." *American Craft* 61, no. 6 (October–November 2001): 60–63, 84.

ROBERT L. BLISS

"Portfolio." *American Craft* 59, no. 3 (June–July 1999): 65.

DALE BROHOLM

Herman, Lloyd E. *Art That Works: Decorative Arts of the Eighties Crafted in America*. Seattle: University of Washington Press, 1990.

Southern Highland Craft Guild. *Chair Show* 4. Asheville, NC: Southern Highland Craft Guild, 2001.

JOHN ERIC BYERS

Falino, Jeannine. "John Eric Byers." *American Craft* 65, no. 2 (April–May 2005): 44–47.

"Portfolio." *American Craft* 53, no. 6 (December 1993–January 1994): 53.

Weisgall, Deborah. *John Eric Byers: A Mid-Career Retrospective*. Brockton, MA: Fuller Craft Museum; New York: Gallery NAGA, 2004.

BYRDCLIFFE CRAFT COLONY

Edwards, Robert. "The Utopias of Ralph Radcliffe Whitehead." *The Magazine Antiques*, January 1985, 267.

ARTHUR ESPENET CARPENTER

Carpenter, Arthur Espenet. "Memoir." In *Furniture Studio: The Heart of the Functional Arts*, edited by John Kelsey and Rick Mastelli, 43–49. Free Union, VA: Furniture Society, 1999.

Jones, Harvey L. *California Woodworking: An Exhibition of Contemporary Handcrafted Furniture*. Oakland: Oakland Museum of Art, 1980.

Landis, Scott. *Conservation by Design*. Providence: Rhode Island School of Design Museum of Art, 1993.

Mastelli, Rick. "Art Carpenter: The Independent Spirit of the Baulines Craftsmen's Guild." *Fine Woodworking*, no. 37 (November–December 1982): 62–68.

Nordness, Lee. *Objects: USA*. New York: Viking Press, 1970.

Renwick Gallery. *Woodenworks; Furniture Objects by Five Contemporary Craftsmen: George Nakashima, Sam Maloof, Wharton Esherick, Arthur Espenet Carpenter, Wendell Castle*. St. Paul: Minnesota Museum of Art, 1972.

Stone, Michael A. *Contemporary American Woodworkers*. Salt Lake City, UT: Peregrine Smith Books, 1986.

WENDELL CASTLE

Castle, Wendell and David Edman. *The Wendell Castle Book of Wood Lamination*. New York: Van Nostrand Reinhold, 1980.

Chastain-Chapman, A. U. "Fine Time: Wendell Castle's Baker's Dozen." *American Craft* 46, no. 2 (April–May 1986): 18–25.

Diamonstein, Barbaralee. *Handmade in America.* New York: Harry N. Abrams, Inc., 1984.

Joseph, Peter. *Angel Chairs: New Work by Wendell Castle.* New York: Peter Joseph Gallery, 1991.

————. *Caligari Presents Recent Work by Wendell Castle.* New York: Peter Joseph Gallery, 1989.

————. *Masterworks.* New York: Peter Joseph Gallery, 1991.

————. *Masterworks Two.* New York: Peter Joseph Gallery, 1994.

Renwick Gallery. *Woodenworks; Furniture Objects by Five Contemporary Craftsmen: George Nakashima, Sam Maloof, Wharton Esherick, Arthur Espenet Carpenter, Wendell Castle.* St. Paul: Minnesota Museum of Art, 1972.

Stone, Michael. *Contemporary American Woodworkers.* Salt Lake City, UT: Peregrine Smith Books, 1986.

Taragin, Davira S., Edward S. Cooke Jr., and Joseph Giovannini. *Furniture by Wendell Castle.* New York, Hudson Hills Press, 1989.

JOHN CEDERQUIST

Danto, Arthur C. and Nancy Princenthal. *The Art of John Cederquist: Reality and Illusion.* Oakland: Oakland Museum of California, 1997.

Emanuelli, Sharon K. "John Cederquist: Deceptions." *American Craft* 44, no. 5 (October–November 1984): 24–27.

Franklin Parrasch Gallery. *John Cederquist: Kosode Built as in a Dream.* New York: Franklin Parrasch Gallery, 2005.

Jones, Harvey L. *California Woodworking: An Exhibition of Contemporary Handcrafted Furniture.* Oakland: Oakland Museum of California, 1980.

Main, Kari M. *Please Be Seated: Contemporary Studio Seating Furniture.* New Haven: Yale University Art Gallery, 1999.

DAVE CHAPMAN

"Portfolio." *American Craft* 57, no. 4 (August–September 1997): 60.

Smith, Paul J. *Objects for Use/Handmade by Design.* New York: Harry N. Abrams, Inc., 2001.

JACOB CRESS

Cranz, Galen. *The Chair: Rethinking Culture, Body, and Design.* New York: W. W. Norton, 1998.

Mobile Museum of Art. *Celebrating the Creative Spirit: Contemporary Southeastern Furniture.* Mobile, AL: Mobile Museum of Art, 1998.

Transformation 2: Contemporary Works in Wood: The Elizabeth R. Raphael Founder's Prize Exhibition, November 12, 1999 through February 26, 2000. Pittsburgh, PA: Society for Contemporary Craft, 1999.

PETER DANKO

Burrows, Dick. "Peter Danko: Props in the Play of Life." *American Craft* 53, no. 2 (Apr/May 1993): 54–57.

Hanks, David A. *Innovative Furniture in America from 1800 to Present.* New York: Horizon Press, 1981.

Kelsey, John. "A One-Piece Chair: They Said It Couldn't Be Done." *Fine Woodworking,* no. 20 (January–February 1980): 46–47.

Smith, Paul J. *Objects for Use/Handmade by Design.* New York; Harry N. Abrams, Inc., 2001.

JOHN DUNNIGAN

Dunnigan, John. "Upholstered Furniture: Filling out the Frame." *Fine Woodworking,* no. 68 (January–February 1988): 52–55.

————. "Understanding Furniture." In *Furniture Studio: The Heart of the Functional Arts,* edited by John Kelsey and Rick Mastelli, 12–23. Free Union, VA: Furniture Society, 1999.

Joseph, Peter. *John Dunnigan, Furniture Maker.* New York: Peter Joseph Gallery, 1991.

————. *Masterworks.* New York: Peter Joseph Gallery, 1991.

————. *Masterworks Two.* New York: Peter Joseph Gallery, 1994.

Temin, Christine. "Poet in Wood: John Dunnigan." *American Craft* 55, no. 6 (December 1995–January 1996): 50–53.

Smith, Paul J. *Objects for Use/Handmade by Design.* New York: Harry N. Abrams, Inc., 2001.

DAVID EBNER

Landis, Scott. *Conservation by Design.* Providence: Rhode Island School of Design Museum of Art, 1993.

Main, Kari M. *Please Be Seated: Contemporary Studio Seating Furniture.* New Haven, Yale University Art Gallery, 1999.

ROBERT ERICKSON

Main, Kari M. *Please Be Seated: Contemporary Studio Seating Furniture.* New Haven: Yale University Art Gallery, 1999.

WHARTON ESHERICK

Bascom, Mansfield. "Wharton Esherick: Dean of American Woodworking." *Craft International,* October, November, December 1985, 22.

Benson, Gertrude. "Wharton Esherick." *Craft Horizons* 19, no. l (January–February 1959): 32–37.

Edwards, Robert and Robert Aibel. *Wharton Esherick, 1877–1970: American Woodworker.* Philadelphia: Moderne Gallery, 1996.

Maloof, Sam and Wendell Castle. "Wharton Esherick 1887–1970." *Craft Horizons* 30, no. 4 (August 1970): 10–17.

Nordness, Lee. *Objects: USA.* New York: Viking Press, 1970.

Renwick Gallery. *Woodenworks; Furniture Objects by Five Contemporary Craftsmen: George Nakashima, Sam Maloof, Wharton Esherick, Arthur Espenet Carpenter, Wendell Castle.* St. Paul: Minnesota Museum of Arts, 1972.

Stone, Michael. *Contemporary American Woodworkers.* Salt Lake City, UT: Peregrine Smith Books, 1986.

Wharton Esherick Museum. *Half a Century in Wood: 1920–1970, The Woodenworks of Wharton Esherick.* Paoli, PA: Wharton Esherick Museum, 1988.

PAUL FREUNDT

Crump, Stephen B. *Studio Furniture: A Fine Art Invitational.* Memphis, TN: Memphis College of Art, 2000.

Southern Highland Craft Guild. *Chair Show 3.* Asheville, NC: Southern Highland Craft Guild, 2000.

TAGE FRID

Frid, Tage. *Furnituremaking, vol. 3, Tage Frid Teaches Woodworking.* Newtown, CT: Taunton Press, 1985.

———. *Joinery, vol. I and Shaping, Veneering, Finishing, vol. 2, Tage Frid Teaches Woodworking.* Newtown, CT: Taunton Press, 1993.

Gilpin, Hank. "Professor Frid." *Fine Woodworking,* no. 146 (winter 2000–2001): 80–85.

Kelsey, John. "Tage Frid: A Talk with the Old Master." *Fine Woodworking,* no 52 (May–June 1985): 66–67.

Stone, Michael. *Contemporary American Woodworkers.* Salt Lake City, UT: Peregrine Smith Books, 1986.

JENNA GOLDBERG

Crump, Stephen B. *Studio Furniture: A Fine Art Invitational.* Memphis, TN: Memphis College of Art, 2000.

JOHN HIGGINBOTHAM

Southern Highland Craft Guild. *Chair Show 3.* Asheville, NC: Southern Highland Craft Guild, 2000.

THOMAS HUCKER

American Craft Museum. *New Handmade Furniture: American Furniture Makers Working in Hardwood.* New York: American Craft Museum, 1979.

Forsyth, Amy. "Jere Osgood and Thomas Hucker: A Tale of Shared Inspiration and a Study in Opposites." *Woodwork,* no. 69 (June 2001): 24–33.

Herman, Lloyd E. *Art That Works: Decorative Arts of the Eighties Crafted in America.* Seattle: University of Washington Press, 1990.

Joseph, Peter. *Masterworks.* New York: Peter Joseph Gallery, 1991.

———. *Masterworks Two.* New York: Peter Joseph Gallery, 1994.

———. *Thomas Hucker.* New York: Peter Joseph Gallery, 1992.

Slivka, Rose. "Thomas Hucker: Counting Angels." *American Craft* 52, no. 3, (June–July 1992): 46–49.

MICHAEL HURWITZ

American Craft Museum. *New Handmade Furniture: American Furniture Makers Working in Hardwood.* New York: American Craft Museum, 1979.

Binzen, Jonathan. "Michael Hurwitz: Furniture-maker's Gift." *Woodwork,* no. 97 (February 2006): 24–31.

Joseph, Peter. *Masterworks.* New York: Peter Joseph Gallery, 1991.

———. *Masterworks Two.* New York: Peter Joseph Gallery, 1994.

———. *Michael Hurwitz.* New York: Peter Joseph Gallery, 1992.

Main, Kari M. *Please Be Seated: Contemporary Studio Seating Furniture.* New Haven: Yale University Art Gallery, 1999.

"New Furniture: In Search of a Contemporary Style." *Fine Woodworking,* no. 30 (September–October 1981): 94–97.

Rush, Michael. "Michael Hurwitz." *American Craft* 57, no. 2 (April–May 1997): 62–66.

DANIEL JACKSON

Corwin, Nancy. "Vital Connections: The Furniture of Daniel Jackson." *American Craft* 50, no. 3 (June–July 1990): 50–55, 74–75.

"Daniel Jackson." *Craft Horizons* 30, no. 3 (May–June 1970): 61.

"Daniel Jackson 1938–1995." *American Craft* 55, no. 5 (October–November 1995): 23.

English Drutt, Helen and Edward S. Cooke Jr. *Daniel Jackson: Dovetailing History.* Philadelphia: The University of the Arts, 2003.

Franklin Parrasch Galleries. *A Tribute to Daniel Jackson.* Washington, DC: Franklin Parrasch Galleries, 1989.

Jackson, Daniel. "Hand Shaping: A Simple Approach to Sculpturing Wood." *Fine Woodworking,* no. 3 (summer 1976): 24–25.

THOMAS LOESER

Austin, Carole, Dyana Curreri-Chadwick, and Ted Cohen. *Nine Decades: The Northern California Craft Movement 1907 to the Present.* San Francisco: San Francisco Museum of Craft & Folk Art, 1993.

Clowes, Judy. "Romancing the Surface." *American Craft* 54, no. 4 (August–September 1994): 54–57, 68.

Gallery at Workbench and Formica Corporation. *Material Evidence: New Color Techniques in Handmade Furniture.* Washington, DC: Smithsonian Institution, 1985.

Horn, Richard. *Memphis, Objects, Furniture, and Patterns.* New York: Simon & Schuster, 1986.

Joseph, Peter. *Masterworks.* New York: Peter Joseph Gallery, 1991.

———. *Masterworks Two.* New York: Peter Joseph Gallery, 1994.

———. *Tom Loeser: Sixty-five Drawers, Eleven Doors and Four Lids.* New York: Peter Joseph Gallery, 1992.

Main, Kari M. *Please Be Seated: Contemporary Studio Seating Furniture.* New Haven: Yale University Art Gallery, 1999.

DANIEL MACK

Hamill, Pete. *Tools as Art: The Hechinger Collection.* New York: Harry N. Abrams, Inc., 1995.

Herman, Lloyd E. *Art That Works: Decorative Arts of the Eighties Crafted in America.* Seattle: University of Washington Press, 1990.

Herman, Lloyd E. and Matthew Kangas. *Trashformations.* Seattle: University of Washington Press, 1998.

Mack, Daniel. *Making Rustic Furniture.* New York: Sterling Publishing Company, 1992.

————. *Rustic Garden Furniture.* Asheville, NC: Lark Books, 2004.

————. *The Rustic Workshop.* Asheville, NC: Lark Books, 1999.

Pepich, Bruce W. *The Aesthetics of Athletics: Artists View Games, Sports and Exercise.* Racine, WI: Charles A. Wustum Museum of Fine Arts, 1994.

KRISTINA MADSEN

Cooke Jr., Edward S. "Women Furniture Makers: From Decorative Designers to Studio Makers." In *Women Designers in the USA 1900–2000*, edited by Pat Kirkham. New Haven: Yale University Press, 2000.

Goodison, Michael, ed. *Sit Up and Take Notice! A Gathering of Artist Benches.* Northampton, MA: Smith College Museum of Art, 2003.

Landis, Scott. *Conservation by Design.* Providence: Rhode Island School of Design Museum of Art, 1993.

Main, Kari M. *Please Be Seated: Contemporary Studio Seating Furniture.* New Haven: Yale University Art Gallery, 1999.

Nelson, Norbert. "Pacific Transfer." *American Craft* 53, no. 6 (December 1993–January 1994): 50–51.

Noll, Terrie. "Return of the Native: Kristina Madsen Revisited." *Woodwork*, no. 51 (June 1998): 20–27.

Olsen, Andrea J. "Kristina Madsen: Textures with a Touch of Class." *Woodwork*, no. 10 (summer 1991): 38–42.

SAM MALOOF

Adamson, Jeremy. *The Furniture of Sam Maloof.* New York and Washington, DC: W. W. Norton and Company in association with the Smithsonian American Art Museum, 2001.

American Craft Museum. *New Handmade Furniture: American Furniture Makers Working in Hardwood.* New York: American Craft Museum, 1979.

Ashton, Shirley. "Maloof: Designer, Craftsman of Furniture." *Craft Horizons* 14, no. 3 (May–June 1954): 15–19.

Diamonstein, Barbaralee. *Handmade in America: Conversations with Fourteen Craftsmasters.* New York: Harry N. Abrams, Inc., 1984.

Herman, Lloyd E. *Art That Works: Decorative Arts of the Eighties Crafted in America.* Seattle: University of Washington Press, 1990.

Jones, Harvey L. *California Woodworking.* Oakland: Oakland Museum of Art, 1980.

Maloof, Sam. *Sam Maloof: Woodworker.* New York: Kodansha International, 1983.

Manhart, Marcia and Tom Manhart. *The Eloquent Object. The Evolution of American Art in Craft Media since 1945.* Tulsa: Philbrook Museum of Art, 1987.

Monroe, Michael. *White House Collection of American Crafts.* New York: Harry N. Abrams, Inc., 1995.

Stone, Michael A. *Contemporary American Woodworkers.* Salt Lake City, UT: Peregrine Smith Books, 1986.

Renwick Gallery. *Woodenworks; Furniture Objects by Five Contemporary Craftsmen: George Nakashima, Sam Maloof, Wharton Esherick, Arthur Espenet Carpenter, Wendell Castle.* St. Paul: Minnesota Museum of Art, 1972.

ALPHONSE MATTIA

Frakes, Mary. "Alphonse Mattia, Rosanne Somerson." *American Craft* 53, no. 6 (December 1993–January 1994): 38–43, 64.

Jeffri, Joan, ed. *The Craftsperson Speaks: Artists in Varied Media Discuss Their Crafts.* New York: Greenwood Press, 1992.

Joseph, Peter. *Alphonse Mattia.* New York: Peter Joseph Gallery, 1993.

————. *Alphonse Mattia: Bookshelves Any Size.* New York: Peter Joseph Gallery, 1993.

————. *Masterworks.* New York: Peter Joseph Gallery, 1991.

————. *Masterworks Two.* New York: Peter Joseph Gallery, 1994.

Landis, Scott. *Conservation by Design.* Providence: Rhode Island School of Design Museum of Art, 1993.

Main, Kari M. *Please Be Seated: Contemporary Studio Seating Furniture.* New Haven: Yale University Art Gallery, 1999.

RORY MCCARTHY

Pearson, Katherine. *American Crafts: A Sourcebook for the Home.* New York: Stewart, Tabori & Chang Publishers, 1983.

JUDY KENSLEY MCKIE

Busch, Akiko. "Judy McKie: Connecting to the World." *American Craft* 54, no. 6 (December 1994–January 1995): 32–35.

Cooke Jr., Edward S. "Women Furniture Makers: From Decorative Designers to Studio Makers." In *Women Designers in the USA 1900–2000*, edited by Pat Kirkham. New Haven: Yale University Press, 2000.

Goodison, Michael, ed. *Sit Up and Take Notice! A Gathering of Artist Benches.* Northampton, MA: Smith College Museum of Art, 2003.

Herman, Lloyd E. *Art That Works: Decorative Arts of the Eighties Crafted in America.* Seattle: University of Washington Press, 1990.

Main, Kari M. *Please Be Seated: Contemporary Studio Seating Furniture.* New Haven: Yale University Art Gallery, 1999.

Mattia, Alphonse. "Judy Kensley McKie." *Workshop*, summer 1983, 10–12.

Smith, Joy Cattanach. "Judy Kensley McKie." *American Craft* 43, no. 6 (December 1983–January 1984): 2–6.

Smith, Paul J. *Objects for Use/Handmade by Design.* New York: Harry N. Abrams, Inc., 2001.

NORMA MINKOWITZ

Whitney, Kathleen, Jane Adlin and David MacFadden. *Portfolio Collection: Norma Minkowitz* (vol 35). Brighton, England: Telos Art Publishing, 2004.

SHINICHI MIYAZAKI

Lydgate, Tony. *The Art of Making Fine Wood Jewelry.* New York: Sterling Publishing, 1998.

"Portfolio." *American Craft* 55, no. 1 (February–March 1995): 58.

GEORGE NAKASHIMA

Beyer, Steven and Matilda McQuaid. *George Nakashima and the Modernist Moment.* Doylestown, PA: James A. Michener Art Museum, 2002.

Kelsey, John. "George Nakashima: For Each Plank There's One Perfect Use." *Fine Woodworking*, no. 14 (January–February 1979): 40–46.

Nakashima, George. "Craftsmanship in Architecture." *Craft Horizons* 16, no. 3 (May–June 1956): 36–31.

————. *The Soul of a Tree: A Woodworker's Reflections.* New York: Kodansha International, 1981.

Nordness, Lee. *Objects: USA.* New York: Viking Press, 1970.

Ostergard, Derek. *George Nakashima: Full Circle.* New York: Weidenfeld & Nicolson in association with American Craft Council, 1989.

Renwick Gallery. *Woodenworks; Furniture Objects by Five Contemporary Craftsmen: George Nakashima, Sam Maloof, Wharton Esherick, Arthur Espenet Carpenter, Wendell Castle.* St. Paul: Minnesota Museum of Art, 1972.

Stone, Michael A. *Contemporary American Woodworkers.* Salt Lake City, UT: Peregrine Smith Books, 1986.

CRAIG NUTT

Connell, Martha Stamm. *Contemporary Works in Woods: Southern Style.* Huntsville: Huntsville Museum of Art, 1990.

Crump, Stephen B. *Studio Furniture: A Fine Art Invitational.* Memphis, TN: Memphis College of Art, 2000.

DiNella, Leslie Blake. *Focus: Four Alabama Artists.* Birmingham, AL: Birmingham Museum of Art, 1989

George, Phyllis. *Craft in America: Celebrating the Creative Work of the Hand.* Fort Worth, TX: The Summit Group, 1993.

Meilach, Dona Z. *Wood Art Today: Furniture, Vessels, Sculpture.* Atglen, PA: Schiffer Publishing, 2004.

Roukes, Nicholas. *Humor in Art: A Celebration of Visual Wit.* Worcester, MA: Davis Publications, 1997.

Smith, Paul J. *Objects for Use/Handmade by Design.* New York: Harry N. Abrams, Inc., 2001.

West, Carroll Van. *Art of Tennessee.* Nashville, TN: Frist Center for the Visual Arts, 2003.

Wood Turning Center. *Wood Turning in North America since 1930.* Philadelphia: Wood Turning Center; New Haven: Yale University Art Gallery, 2001.

JERE OSGOOD

Crump, Stephen B. *Studio Furniture: A Fine Art Invitational.* Memphis, TN: Memphis College of Art, 2000.

Nordness, Lee. *Objects: USA.* New York: Viking Press, 1970.

Osgood, Jere. "Jere Osgood." In *The Penland Book of Woodworking*, edited by Thomas Stender. Asheville, NC: Lark Books, 2006.

————. "Meditation on the Desk." In *Furniture Studio: Tradition in Contemporary Furniture*, edited by Rick Mastelli and John Kelsey. Free Union, VA: Furniture Society, 2001.

————. "Tapered Lamination." *Fine Woodworking*, no. 14 (January–February 1979): 48–51.

Somerson, Rosanne, "Perfect Sweep." *American Craft* 45, no. 3 (June–July 1985): 30–34.

Stone, Michael A. *Contemporary American Woodworkers.* Salt Lake City, UT: Peregrine Smith Books, 1986.

ALBERT PALEY

Adcock, Craig. *Albert Paley: Sculpture, Drawings, Graphics & Decorative Arts.* Jacksonville: Florida State University Museum of Fine Arts, 2001.

Bell, Robert. *Design Visions.* Perth, Art Gallery of Western Australia, 1992.

————. *Transformations: The Language of Craft.* Canberra: National Gallery of Australia, 2005.

Gorlin, Debra. *Albert Paley: The Art of Metal.* Springfield, MA: Museum of Fine Arts, 1985.

Horn, John, Michael Monroe, and Townsend Wolf. *Living with Form: The Horn Collection of Contemporary Crafts.* Little Rock, AR: Bradley Publishing, 1999.

Hunter-Stiebel, Penelope and Peter Joseph. *Albert Paley: Organic Logic.* New York: Peter Joseph Gallery, 1994.

Joseph, Peter. *Baroque Modernism: New Work by Albert Paley.* New York: Peter Joseph Gallery, 1992.

————. *Masterworks.* New York: Peter Joseph Gallery, 1991.

————. *Masterworks Two.* New York: Peter Joseph Gallery, 1994.

Kangas, Matthew. *Craft and Concept: The Rematerialization of the Art Object*. New York: Midmarch Arts Press, 2006.

Lucie-Smith, Edward. *The Art of Albert Paley: Iron, Bronze, and Steel*. New York: Harry N. Abrams, Inc., 1996.

McCreight, Tim. *Design Language*. Portland, ME: Brynmorgen Press, 2006.

Sobieszek, Robert. "Albert Paley, Romantic in Metal." *American Craft* 40, no. 2 (April–May 1980): 12–17.

Trilling, James. *Ornament: A Modern Perspective*. Seattle: University of Washington Press, 2003.

STEPHEN PERRIN

"Portfolio." *American Craft* 56, no. 1 (February–March 1996): 59.

TIMOTHY PHILBRICK

Joseph, Peter. *Masterworks*. New York: Peter Joseph Gallery, 1991.

———. *Masterworks Two*. New York: Peter Joseph Gallery, 1994.

———. *Timothy Philbrick: New Furniture*. New York: Peter Joseph Gallery, 1992.

Landis, Scott. *Conservation by Design*. Providence: Rhode Island School of Design Museum of Art, 1993.

Pearson, Katherine. *American Crafts: A Source-book for the Home*. New York: Stewart, Tabori & Chang Publishers, 1983.

Philbrick, Timothy. "Tall Chests: The Art of Proportioning." *Fine Woodworking*, no. 9 (Winter 1977): 39–43.

PETER PIEROBON

Smith, Paul J. *Objects for Use/Handmade by Design*. New York: Harry N. Abrams, Inc., 2001.

PETER PITTMAN

Adamson, Glenn. "The Next Moment in Studio Furniture." In *Tradition in Contemporary Furniture*, edited by Rick Mastelli and John Kelsey, 100–105. Free Union, VA: The Furniture Society, 2001.

Mobile Museum of Art. *Celebrating the Creative Spirit: Contemporary Southeastern Furniture*. Mobile, AL: Mobile Museum of Art, 1998.

Society of Contemporary Craft. *Transformation 2: Contemporary Works in Wood: The Elizabeth R. Raphael Founder's Prize Exhibition, November 12, 1999 through February 26, 2000*. Pittsburgh, PA: Society for Contemporary Craft, 1999.

KIM SCHMAHMANN

Rosen, Michael. *Turning Words, Spinning Worlds: Chapters in Organizational Ethnography*. Abingdon, England: Routledge, 2000.

JOANNE SHIMA

Main, Kari M. *Please Be Seated: Contemporary Studio Seating Furniture*. New Haven: Yale University Art Gallery, 1999.

RANDY SHULL

Landis, Scott. *Conservation by Design*. Providence: Rhode Island School of Design Museum of Art, 1993.

McLaughlin, Jean W. *The Nature of Craft and the Penland Experience*. New York: Sterling Publishing Co., 2004.

Smith, Paul J. *Objects for Use/Handmade by Design*. New York: Harry N. Abrams, Inc., 2001.

TOMMY SIMPSON

Davidson, Marshall. "Wooden Wiles of Tommy Simpson." *Craft Horizons* 38, no. 1 (January–February 1978): 45–47, 67.

Herman, Lloyd E. *Art That Works: Decorative Arts of the Eighties Crafted in America*. Seattle: University of Washington Press, 1990.

Kangas, Matthew. *Breaking Barriers: Recent American Craft*. New York: American Craft Museum, 1995.

Long, Robert. "Tommy Simpson: Tapping Into Universal Memory." *American Craft* 65, no. 5 (October–November 2005): 60–63.

Nordness, Lee. *Objects: USA*. New York: Viking Press, 1970.

Roukes, Nicholas. *Artful Jesters: Innovators of Visual Wit and Humor*. Berkeley: Ten-Speed Press, 2003.

Simpson, Tommy. *Two Looks to Home: The Art of Tommy Simpson*. Boston: Little, Brown & Company, 1999.

Smith, Paul J. *Objects for Use/Handmade by Design*. New York: Harry N. Abrams, Inc., 2001.

EVERT SODERGREN

Landis, Scott. "Design in Context: Woodworkers of the Northwest." In *Fine Woodworking Design Book Five*. Newtown, CT: Taunton Press, 1990.

Portland Art Museum, *Works in Wood by Northwest Artists*. Portland, OR: Portland Art Museum, 1976.

ROSANNE SOMERSON

American Craft Museum. *New Handmade Furniture: American Furniture Makers Working in Hardwood*. New York: American Craft Museum, 1979.

Edward S. Cooke Jr. "Women Furniture Makers: From Decorative Designers to Studio Makers." In *Women Designers in the USA 1900–2000*, edited by Pat Kirkham (New Haven: Yale University Press, 2000).

Crump, Stephen B. *Studio Furniture: A Fine Art Invitational*. Memphis, TN: Memphis College of Art, 2000.

Frakes, Mary. "Alphonse Mattia, Rosanne Somerson." *American Craft* 53, no. 6 (December 1993–January 1994): 38–43, 64.

Goodison, Michael, ed. *Sit Up and Take Notice! A Gathering of Artist Benches*. Northampton, MA: Smith College Museum of Art, 2003.

Joseph, Peter. *Masterworks.* New York: Peter Joseph Gallery, 1991.

———. *Masterworks Two.* New York: Peter Joseph Gallery, 1994.

———. *Rosanne Somerson: Earthly Delights.* New York: Peter Joseph Gallery, 1993.

Landis, Scott. *Conservation by Design.* Providence: Rhode Island School of Design Museum of Art, 1993.

JAY STANGER

Gallery at Workbench and Formica Corporation. *Material Evidence: New Color Techniques in Handmade Furniture.* Washington, DC: Smithsonian Institution, 1985.

Kraus, Bill. *Contemporary Crafts for the Home: Featuring Winners of the American Crafts Awards.* New York: Kraus Sikes, Inc., 1990.

Mayer, Barbara. *Contemporary American Craft Art: A Collector's Guide.* Salt Lake City, UT: Peregrine Smith Books, 1988.

Taragin, Davira S. *Contemporary Crafts and the Saxe Collection.* New York: Hudson Hills Press, 1993.

ROY SUPERIOR

Ferrin, Leslie. *Teapots Transformed: Exploration of an Object.* Madison, WI: Guild Publishing, 2000.

Hamill, Pete. *Tools as Art: The Hechinger Collection.* New York: Harry N. Abrams, Inc., 1995.

Roukes, Nicholas. *Artful Jesters: Innovators of Visual Wit and Humor.* Berkeley: Ten-Speed Press, 2003.

Simpson, Tommy. *Hand and Home: The Homes of American Craftsmen.* Boston: Little Brown & Co., 1994.

JON SUTTER

"Portfolio." *American Craft* 61, no. 2 (Apr 2001): 71.

Siegel, Kathran. "Art Furniture." In *Furniture Studio: Tradition in Contemporary Furniture*, edited by Rick Mastelli and John Kelsey, 84–99. Free Union, VA: Furniture Society, 2001.

BOB TROTMAN

Connell, Martha Stamm. *Contemporary Works in Woods: Southern Style.* Huntsville, AL: Huntsville Museum of Art, 1990.

Herman, Lloyd E. *Art That Works: Decorative Arts of the Eighties Crafted in America.* Seattle: University of Washington Press, 1990.

Landis, Scott. *Conservation by Design.* Providence: Rhode Island School of Design Museum of Art, 1993.

MacDougal, Frances M. "Philosophical Furniture." Southern Accents, November–December 1995, 117.

Trotman, Bob. *Bob Trotman: A Retrospective of Furniture and Sculpture.* Raleigh, NC: The Center, 1994.

ROBERT WHITLEY

Conn, Carol. "Robert Whitley: Working with Truth in Wood." *American Craft* 40, no. 2 (April–May 1980): 24–27, 84.

Eshelman, Kristian. "Master Craftsman Robert Whitley." *Woodwork,* no. 41 (October 1996): 30–37.

ROB WOMACK

Maryland Art Place. *Furniture as Art: Room as Illusion.* Baltimore: Maryland Art Place, 1986.

McDonough Museum of Art. *Sleight of Hand.* Youngstown, OH: McDonough Museum of Art, 2004.

RICK WRIGLEY

Crump, Stephen B. *Studio Furniture: A Fine Art Invitational.* Memphis, TN: Memphis College of Art, 2000.

Grow, Lawrence. *Modern Style: A Catalogue of Contemporary Design.* Pittstown, NJ: Main Street Press, 1985.

Jencks, Charles. *Postmodernism: New Classicism in Art and Architecture.* New York: Rizzoli, 1987.

Kraus, Bill. *Contemporary Crafts for the Home: Featuring Winners of the American Crafts Awards.* New York: Kraus Sikes, Inc., 1990.

Scheinman, Pamela. "Dialogue with Architecture: Rick Wrigley." *American Craft* 48, no. 3 (June–July 1988): 60–61.

Photography credits

MILDRED BALDWIN

pages 26 (top and bottom), 35, and 65

LEA CHRISTIANO

page 73

MICHAEL FISCHER

pages 18 (top left) and 107

COURTESY OF JENNA GOLDBERG

pages 99 and 204

BRUCE MILLER

cover and pages 12, 25 (top right), 30–31, 33, 45, 49, 55, 56, 57, 58–9, 60, 68, 74, 77, 81, 87, 91, 93, 95, 104–5, 109, 111, 118–9, 125, 127, 129, 130, 131, 133, 135, 138, 143, 148, 149, 152–3, 155, 161, 162, 167, 169, 171, 175, 183, 187, 191, 197, and 199

EDWARD OWEN

pages 144–5

GENE YOUNG

title page and pages 6, 25 (top left and bottom), 36–7, 38, 39, 40, 42, 43 (top and bottom), 47, 51, 52–3, 62, 63, 67, 70, 71, 78–9, 82, 85, 88, 89, 97, 100, 101, 102–3, 113, 114, 121, 122, 123, 141, 147, 151, 154, 157, 159, 165, 172, 173, 176, 178, 180, 181, 185, 189, 194–5, 201, and 203